This program was originally inspired by my experiences while working with a courageous group of cancer patients. These intuitively wise individuals taught me that the quality of living and dying depends on one's capacity to both experience and balance intense emotions. Later I discovered that this same principle applied to all our lives, and not just those whose struggles are illness related.

The passage from fear to wisdom and hope is one that requires us to connect with feelings that we may dislike or disapprove of. However, this experience not only frees us from patterns that limit health but transforms our lives in ways that strengthen us physically, emotionally, and spiritually. Beyond fear lies power, freedom, and love.

JEANNE SEGAL, PH.D.

''The prize offered here is nothing less than transformation. . . . Segal covers the various 'heavies' of psychic blocking (e.g., pain, fear, anger, sadness). . . . The book's message is simple and compelling: Become aware of your body's physical responses to stress, and begin to reconnect with your essential core.''

New Age MAGAZINE

Also by Jeanne Segal, Ph.D.:

FEELING GREAT: A Personal Program to Speed
  Healing and Enhance Wellness

LIVING BEYOND FEAR

A COURSE FOR COPING WITH
THE EMOTIONAL ASPECTS OF
LIFE-THREATENING ILLNESSES

FOR PATIENTS, FAMILIES AND HEALTH-
CARE PROFESSIONALS

Jeanne Segal, Ph.D.

BALLANTINE BOOKS · NEW YORK

To Robert Segal, beloved husband and helpmate,
who makes my celebration of life
as sacred to him as his own.

Copyright © 1984, 1989 by Jeanne Segal

All rights reserved under International and Pan-American Copyright Conventions. Published in the United States of America by
Ballantine Books, a division of Random House, Inc., New York,
and simultaneously in Canada by Random House of Canada Limited, Toronto. Originally published, in different form, by Newcastle
Publishing, Inc. in 1984.

ISBN 0-345-36055-9

in the United States of America

e Books Edition: November 1989

CONTENTS

Introduction   1

PART I   PREPARING FOR CHANGE   13
  CHAPTER 1 *Laying the Foundation*   15
  CHAPTER 2 *Learning to Feel . . . Again*   32

PART II   OPENING   55
  CHAPTER 3 *Criticism, Judgment, and
             Punishment*   57
  CHAPTER 4 *Observation and Acceptance*   72
  CHAPTER 5 *Wanting vs. Needing*   91

PART III FACING FEAR   109
  CHAPTER 6 *Learning to Live with Fear*   111
  CHAPTER 7 *The Living Beyond Fear Process:
             Ride the Wild Horse*   129

PART IV   DEEPENING   149
  CHAPTER 8 *Pain and Grief*   151
  CHAPTER 9 *Rage*   170
  CHAPTER 10 *Numbing*   186

PART V   AWAKENING   199
  CHAPTER 11 *Life After Fear*   201

EXERCISES

PART I   13

  CHAPTER 1   15
    Freeze!   28
    Creating A Personal Energy Scanner   28
    Observing the Difference Between
    Goals and Processes   30
  CHAPTER 2   32
    The Part Feelings Play in My Life   41
    The Nature of My Feelings   42
    How Does Physical and Emotional
    Experience Shape My Life?   43
    Where Do I Feel the Feelings?   44
    Inventory for Turning Fear into Intimacy   45
    Extending My Range of Feeling
    Awareness   46
    Breathing Life into Feeling   47
    Scanning for Feeling   48
    Moving to Music   49
    Blindfold Exercise   50
    Stretch   51
    Focus on Sensual Feeling   51
    Sound Off!   52
    Feelings About My Mate   54

                                  55
                                  57
    nk) Is Too (Blank)!   67

In My Opinion! 68
Punishment Assessment 69
CHAPTER 4 72
Interior Assessment 84
Secondary Gains 85
Telling the (Oops) Truth 85
Assessing the Truth 86
Who Are You? 86
Watching the Picture Show Inside
Your Head 87
My Face—the Mirror of My Inner World 88
Is the Universe Friendly? 90
CHAPTER 5 91
Desires Assessment 104
What I Can't Live Without 104
What Do I Want? What Do I Need? 105
Reflecting On Values 107
Creating a Witness to the Choices I Make 108
Understanding Values 108

PART III 109
CHAPTER 6 111
What Do I Fear 123
Interpersonal Fears Quiz 124
Overcoming the Fear of Intensity 125
Following Fear to Its Natural Conclusion 125
Learning From Nightmares 126
Facing the Fear of Death 127
CHAPTER 7 129
Ride the Wild Horse 132

PART IV   149
  CHAPTER 8   151
    Pain and Grief Inventory   162
    Pain—How do I Know Thee   164
    Pain by Other Names   165
    Your Relationship to Loss   166
    Creative Applications of Pain   167
  CHAPTER 9   170
    Rage Inventory   181
    My Feelings About Anger   183
    Exploring My Rage   184
  CHAPTER 10   186
    Numbing Inventory   195
    Gaining Insight About Numbing   197
    "Socially Acceptable" Numbing   197

Introduction

> *"If you do not get it from yourself,*
> *where will you go for it?"*
> —Zenrin
> *The Gospel According to Zen*

"Why me?"

"Why me?" Like a broken record I kept asking, "What's wrong with me? Why am I so angry, so depressed? Why do I feel so empty so much of the time?"

I had "made it." I was young, attractive, socially acceptable, and financially secure. I lived surrounded by a loving husband, family, and a beautiful home overlooking the sea. I had my art and my freedom. I had it all, and that's precisely what made my dissatisfaction so maddening and my unhappiness humiliating.

When I was active—working, painting, mothering—I felt relatively content. Activity distracted me, but I could not stay occupied twenty-four hours a day. My brief attempts at obliterating the emptiness that filled my life were great disappointments. Alcohol or drugs only succeeded in making me sleepy or nauseated.

I was reaching the end of my emotional rope when a dear friend suggested I join her as she pursued a master's degree in psychology. "Go back to school," she said. "Stop whining and complaining. Think about something besides yourself." I had always loved learning; perhaps in a psychological setting I would find something to help me.

While pursuing a formal education, I also rushed to experience every therapeutic modality available. With a personal philosophy of "experience informs," I threw myself into the numerous therapeutic offerings of the human potential movement. My family and friends reeled from my pursuit of each new "therapy of the month." I had insatiable enthusiasm. I was driven.

The potential of each new therapy buoyed me up and seduced me into thinking that "this was the one"—but ultimately each one left me flat. It also became clear that no matter how profound their insights were, my teachers, counselors, and colleagues all suffered in various ways. This indicated to me that they had not found "it" either.

Could it be that life is just hard and full of pain? Is this simply the human condition? Is unhappiness a depressing fact of life? Try as I might, I could not—and would not—accept the premise that this was all there was. I retained a very clear memory of what life had felt like when I was a child. I remembered my state of endless enthusiasm and expectancy. Joy had been a real and major part of my life, along with occasional tears and disappointments. Was this passionate experience of life lost simply by growing up? No! Something I couldn't explain kept insisting that the joy I remembered was more real than the emptiness I now felt. In addition, every so often in moments of creative outpouring or intimate exchanges with Robert and our children, I felt filled to overflowing once again.

My husband, Robert, decided to enroll in a doctoral

program in health psychology. Again, I was asked to join someone in the pursuit of a graduate degree, and again I accepted. The program offered us the opportunity to go off on a spiritual retreat, and although I never had meditated, prayed, chanted, or considered myself a religious type, I was as curious as ever. Surprisingly, doors to spiritual awareness did open to me, and I experienced myself as part of the greater whole, far more than just the encapsulated separateness I had perceived myself to be. This state of awareness assuaged my fear of death and prepared me for the next major step in my transformational journey.

My doctoral project involved working with cancer patients and their families. Here was suffering so immediate and compelling that I lost all awareness of my personal pain while caring about theirs. Counseling demanded such total presence that I was able to forget myself completely. My personal experiences with despair enabled me to empathize with and support families going through their own private hell, even though my agony seemed far less tangible than theirs.

All of the people that I counseled were expected to die within a very short time. As my work progressed, I began to question and eventually research the reasons why some patients survived. Psychosocial intervention was contemplated only as a last resort after all medical possibilities had first been exhausted. What was so surprising was that not only were many of these patients able to add many months of quality living to their lives, but a few completely defied the odds and are living today!

Those I sought to serve ended up serving me by showing me that people who were willing to experience their most dreaded fears and feelings somehow tapped a resource that brought renewal into their lives. If those who

were desperately ill and exhausted by months of chemotherapy and radiation could find the strength and the courage to confront their emotional bogeymen, couldn't I find
the courage to face the depths of emotional pain that
sucked the joy out of my life? My patients had shown me
that it is possible to really change, not in years but in
months, sometimes weeks, when motivation is great
enough. People fighting for their lives cannot afford to
waste time or energy. There can be no partial commitment. I, too, decided to make a commitment. I vowed
that I would face anything and everything about myself,
no matter how ugly or disturbing, and become an unre-
lenting, uncritical observer of all my feelings including
those that terrified me.

Each day I set aside time to be alone even though it was
very difficult, because there appeared to be so many distractions. I persevered, however, and experimented with
a variety of methods and techniques until I uncovered a
process that consistently evoked a powerful emotional or
physical reaction. I worked with these responses, going
deep into the core of them, returning to my sense of dread,
my anxiety, my despair day after day. I guarded this time
by myself zealously, but at its end I would get up and
return to my daily routine.

Over time, I discovered that the experience of feeling
physical and emotional intensity terrified me and thus I
had created an almost singularly "mental" existence.
Control, rather than love or joy, had been my real objective. I didn't feel my feelings—I thought about them and
used my emotions to manipulate others. I had always assumed that I was "in touch with my emotions" because
I could "express my anger." Wrong! My anger was just
a façade staged and directed from the bridge of the nose

up. When I attuned to what I felt in my body, I rarely experienced anything other than emptiness or fear from the bridge of the nose down. There were times, especially at the beginning, when I thought that I would die or that my mind would crack and my intelligence would spill into the gutter. No wonder I had been so controlling: I was terrified!

However, as I continued to make myself focus on all that I had experienced throughout my body, I also began to experience positive feelings.

The vulnerable, feeling part of me that I had been so fearful of facing eventually surfaced as a wise friend! My "feeling self" saw through my masquerades and indulgences and past my insecurities and sense of being overwhelmed. This self showed me a way that brought peace and tranquility as well as a greatly extended capacity to forgive and love. Surprisingly, my vulnerable, feeling self not only supported but also improved upon the mental self that had so resisted the entry of "feeling" into my life. I was sharper and more focused than I had been in years. The vast resource of my energy, long held down by continuing resistance to my emotions, was now beginning to surface in ways that energized and enriched all my experiences. I began to understand the sad irony of Franklin Delano Roosevelt's observation: "All we have to fear is fear itself."

1986

With the initial publication of *Living Beyond Fear* in 1984, I had opportunities to conduct seminars and workshops throughout the United States and abroad with people who were experiencing life-threatening crises in a great variety of settings. I taught and tested the LIVING BE-YOND FEAR (LBF) process with large and small groups, sometimes speaking through interpreters, as I did in Russia and Japan. The more people I worked with, the more I came to trust and believe in the LIVING BEYOND FEAR process.

One of the most exciting validations of the LIVING BEYOND FEAR process was provided by a successful two-year longitudinal study undertaken by Napon, a very large Japanese insurance company. For two years, they followed the progress of thirty-five directors who had been trained to integrate the LIVING BEYOND FEAR process into both their personal and professional lives. All of those individuals not only continued to use the process themselves, but had introduced it to those they supervised and made it an ongoing part of the work setting.

LIVING BEYOND THE FEAR OF AIDS

I had seen my first AIDS patient as early as 1983, although at that time no one foresaw the health crisis that was to come. Within the next few years, however, more and more people asked me if the LIVING BEYOND FEAR process of psychosocial and psychospiritual intervention that I practiced could also apply to work with AIDS patients. My immediate intuition was, "Yes, it probably would." But without exploring the process with more than a few AIDS-related cases, I knew I could not be completely certain. As more and more individuals were challenged with AIDS, my attention began to shift to the overwhelming need for emotional support experienced by AIDS patients and their families.

The expansion of the focus of my work was gradual.

Initially, I offered free short-term group sessions to individuals with ARC or who were HIV positive, and occasionally included those diagnosed as having advanced symptoms of AIDS who had the strength and clarity of mind to come to my office and practice the LIVING BEYOND FEAR process. The results were extremely gratifying. Those who chose to work with the process did it with an energy and enthusiasm and at a rate of personal growth I had not encountered before.

My education was not limited to a deeper understanding of the physical, social, and psychological aspects of AIDS—I also learned about the accompanying social illnesses such as homophobia and xenophobia. If ever there was a disease with roots in the very fabric of society, it is AIDS. AIDS gives all of us—heterosexuals and homosexuals alike—an opportunity to learn, heal, and evolve. I believe that failure to meet the challenge of AIDS might well lead society as a whole toward an untimely end—an end not necessarily connected with the virus itself.

TESTING THE PROCESS ON MY OWN LIFE

Over the years, I'd had a few personal opportunities to use the LIVING BEYOND FEAR process in my own behalf. For example, in 1978, I severed the tip of my elbow in a skating accident. At that time, I successfully combined the LIVING BEYOND FEAR process with visualization in order to glue back a nickle-sized piece of bone to the end of my elbow with scar tissue. The piece of bone was lodged in my upper arm, and an orthopedic surgeon had agreed to postpone surgery in order to allow me to guide the bone fragment back to its proper place by means of this technique. Within a few weeks, the bone was in place and I had thus avoided a surgical process that would have left my arm with a restricted range of motion.

Finally, as I entered my fiftieth year in 1988, I had an opportunity to test the validity of the LIVING BEYOND FEAR process on a major physical illness of my own. That year, I suddenly began to hemorrhage, although I had no previous history of gynecological problems. I assumed it would stop, but it did not, and I grew increasingly weak. Blood transfusions are not very popular these days, but after six weeks I was told that my options were either blood transfusions or a full hysterectomy. Moreover, I was cautioned that if I didn't make my mind up soon there would be no options left at all!

By this time, I was not only physically enervated but also mentally impaired. Just thinking had become a real effort. Surprisingly, it had not occurred to me to use the process until this point in my crisis. Perhaps I was so accustomed to the role of healer that, in my weakened condition, I failed to realize that it was I who needed healing. Using the LIVING BEYOND FEAR process, I checked out the cause of my problem and gave myself a couple of weeks to affect it with the methods I had so often trained others to use.

I asked both my body and my mind to help me see where my life lacked harmony. What was I missing? What possible need was I ignoring? I didn't do a number on myself and ask how I had "created" the disease. Whatever part I had played was not conscious or deliberate. Insight—not blame—was what I sought. The insight that came gave me permission to stop pushing myself. It directed me to pay attention to my own needs as well as the world's needs—and my need cried out for time to engage in my spiritual interests.

As I attuned to my physical sensations, I discovered what felt like intense internal activity or raw energy circulating throughout my body. These perceptions had nothing to do with my heart rate or pulse. They were much stronger. A friend suggested that I harness this energy and direct it to the source of the bleeding. In spite of my personal and professional experiences, I was still amazed when this process actually halted the flow of blood. I had known that others could do this, but, until I did it myself, I hadn't been sure that I could!

In the months that followed, I continued to successfully control the hemorrhaging by setting aside several short periods of time during the day for internal focus—something I had wanted to do for years but had felt was self-indulgent. The process sharpened both my reasoning and my intuition. I felt the need to explore various opportunities for speeding recovery. Thus, I also began to employ alternative medical regimens intended to heal the physical causes of the problem. Each of these I tested by attuning to the feeling sensations in my body and asking the following question: "Are my strength and energy improving?"

Today, my health is better than it has ever been. It seems clear to me that work with the LIVING BEYOND FEAR process paved the way for my own personal recovery. Moreover, what began as a frightening and traumatic personal event has initiated a commitment on my part to maintain a more consistent relationship with my physical body and its ongoing messages. The result is that a change has taken place—one that is rooted in the change of a decade ago when I first experimented with learning how to experience my feelings fully. At that time, I uncovered a world that enabled me to push past the emotional blocks that were suffocating me. This time, I discovered a world of subtle energy that has enabled me to heal more rapidly and to experience a palpable sense of connection to the life force.

WHO WILL BENEFIT FROM THIS BOOK?

My work in the health field and my travels throughout the world have taught me how common an experience it is to search outwardly for what we need, hoping someone or something will give us the answers we desperately seek. In doing so, many find themselves data rich but life poor. THE LIVING BEYOND FEAR process is for anyone who feels stressed or overwhelmed by serious health issues. It is also for anyone with the courage to face their vulnerability, their humanity, and their divinity. It can be a guide to regaining energy and empowerment for people who are ill or fearful of becoming ill; and it can be a supportive tool for individuals whose pain, stress, or feelings of being overwhelmed, are triggered by the experience of caring for seriously ill patients or loved ones. This book will also be very useful for those who, having been touched by death, are reclaiming life.

Anyone who has abandoned or exhausted the offerings of simplistic solutions when faced with complex and difficult situations can also find support in these pages. People who are ready to make a long-term commitment to themselves and to a quality of living that makes life wholly worthwhile will also benefit from this process.

This book will be particularly helpful to those who suffer from any of the autoimmune diseases that continue to proliferate at an alarming rate—including cancer and AIDS. Hard scientific data now substantiates the cause-

and-effect relationship between the nervous system and the autoimmune system—and the relationship between physical/emotional feeling awareness and autoimmune health is one of the central concerns of the LIVING BEYOND FEAR process. This is why I believe a book about feelings is central to today's health issues.

LIVING BEYOND FEAR is a response to the questions: *"How can I remain empowered in the midst of relentless stress, crisis, and suffering?" "What does it take to transform the limitations I encounter into an abundance of purpose, meaning, and love?"*

Finally, this is a book for anyone wishing to live a fuller, more passionate and vital life. But beware! It is a book that will make demands on you. It is a book that may change not only your point of view—it may radically change your life.

PART I

Preparing for a Change

CHAPTER 1

Laying the Foundation

"Trust in God, but tie your camel to a tree."
—Unknown

FAST RELIEF VS. SELF-DISCOVERY

When pain strikes, of course we want relief, and we are told we can have it instantly! The illusion of an immediate cure for even our most distressing and chronic of problems has been perpetuated by doctors, the pharmaceutical industry, and modern advertising. Experience, however, teaches us that such remedies are, for the most part, non-existent. There are fewer and fewer "magic bullets" for today's truly distressing and difficult health problems, and this fact is reinforced by medical science as well as practical knowledge. Space age technology has been able to put men on the moon, but it has not been able to find a cure for the proliferating number of chronic or degenerative diseases, nor for cancer, AIDS, or a host of other autoimmune diseases.

Since the turn of the century, many health problems have been solved, but seemingly no faster than previously rare diseases such as lung cancer have become common, or new diseases like AIDS or venereal warts have emerged. In developed countries, people no longer die prematurely of infectious diseases like polio or tuberculosis; instead, life is prolonged, often painfully so. Infants now survive their first years of life, yet today young adults encounter a multiplying host of autoimmune diseases that were thought to be confined to old age in bygone days. Social diseases like drug, alcohol, and child abuse flourish at all levels of society, leaving in their wake a devastating tide of personal destruction. And with rising medical costs and the alarming rate at which health-care institutions are closing down, medical support for serious health problems is becoming increasingly unavailable or out of reach. In light of such facts, can we honestly hold onto the belief that America is growing healthier and healthier?

If prompt medical care isn't going to deliver us from suffering, is anything? Perhaps you're hoping that this book will suggest a cure-all. It won't! There is no single answer or solution that benefits everyone. Healing is an individual process and, therefore, penetrating self-knowledge holds more true promise for alleviating suffering and regaining health than magic bullets. This approach to health, in which the individual accepts responsibility and actively participates in his or her healing, is the foundation of LIVING BEYOND FEAR. It is also the subject of my favorite healing arts story, which took place at Epidaurus, the birthplace of both Western medicine and the holistic approach to health.

EPIDAURUS

The ancient Greek healing shrine and temple at Epidaurus was dedicated to Asclepius, the demigod of healing and medicine. It flourished from the sixth century B.C. to the fifth century A.D. Healing at that time was believed to include both personal and psychospiritual elements, and therefore no distinction was made between the role of a physician and that of a priest. Supplicants would undertake a healing journey to Epidaurus if either a physical or an emotional health problem arose.

Once there, they entered into a process of individual self-discovery that began with making ritual offerings. This ritual held up a mirror to hidden parts of one's personality by requiring the "patient" to place an offering at the feet of each and every deity represented at Epidaurus. And the deities were numerous—there were gods and goddesses that stood for every imaginable human attribute. One was encouraged to pick favorites and perhaps to make more generous offerings to them—for example to Apollo, the solar deity who represented wisdom and refinement. However, one had better not completely forget the other gods—let's say Dionysus, the god of ecstasy and drunken revelry—because an offended deity could become angry and vengeful. Illness was thought to be initiated by the neglect of disowned or disliked attributes or shadows personified by the deities. This ritual brought home the fact that important parts of life might not be receiving proper attention.

The next part of the ritual necessitated sleeping on the marble floor of the great hall at Epidaurus. Here you were to incubate dreams that would indicate the course the healing would take. A serious impediment, however, lay in the way. Harmless snakes were released in the dark to crawl among the sleepers. These were living symbols of the snakes twisting around the winged staff of Hermes, god of healing and of deep communication, that gave us the symbol of medicine we recognize today as the caduceus. It must have taken a well-developed ability to overcome fear to even close one's eyes at Epidaurus! Finally, once the rituals were completed, one was permitted to consult the physician/priest.

Of course I can't testify to the cure rate of the people who completed these healing rituals, but based on experience, I imagine it to have been high. Therefore, in the spirit of recovery and renewal that takes us down the path of self-discovery, inspired by the journey of the ancients to Epidaurus, let us begin to lay a foundation for understanding the processes that will initiate your own healing journey.

INSIGHTS GLEANED FROM THE HOLISTIC HEALTH MOVEMENT OF THE 20TH CENTURY

In the last two decades, we have witnessed the worldwide rebirth of a holistic approach to health. This movement has been built not only on alternative approaches to medicine, but equally on humanistic and existential values that celebrate individual empowerment. This renaissance has already provided a number of sobering axioms to those of us who have been working in this manner for over a decade.

You Can't Write Off Any Approach

All programs and techniques work for some of the people some of the time, but not all of the people, and certainly not all of the time. Any one or combination of traditional or alternative techniques, therapies, or programs will work for some individuals and be relatively useless to others. Moreover, there is no way to objectively match an individual with the "perfect" health recovery program. The match, such as it is, is initiated by the patient, who may or may not take responsibility for monitoring the results. This is why the practice of medicine has been called an art rather than a science.

Others Can't Do It For Us

It has become clear that the mechanistic approach to health doesn't work. People are not machines to be handed over to a doctor or therapist of any orientation for readjustment and overhauls. We certainly can benefit from the knowledge, wisdom, and experience of others, but such benefits support rather than assure health and healing. Helpers and healers focus on the objective rather than subjective aspects of disease. They can care, comfort, and offer possible solutions, but they can never know more about the patient than that individual knows about himself or herself. The more responsibility the patient takes for assessing the value of a particular course of treatment, the more this is the case.

Health Is a Process

There is no such thing as a state of health that stays put. What works or is good for us today may not work or be good for us tomorrow or five years from now. One doesn't *attain* health, one *maintains* the process of health. This means that lasting recovery requires a commitment to keep changing in positive directions. Seen from this perspective, the frequently quoted statement of those who survive life-threatening diseases isn't as shocking as it first appears to be. These individuals often say, "My illness has changed my life for the better!"

What kind of a process is health? This question has been debated vigorously by a variety of holistic health practitioners. One group equates health with the ability to formulate positive thoughts and intentions. This group attempts to influence health through positive reprogramming techniques such as visualization and affirmation. Another group stresses the need to correct physiological and biological imbalances through alternative medical interventions or by such means as diet, vitamin and/or mineral supplements, movement and exercise. Still others have stressed the need for spiritual development and the ability to attune with God or the universal life force.

For many years it has been anyone's guess as to where the proper balance of emphasis should be placed in the body, mind, spirit equation, but recently a new field of science called psychoneuroimmunology has uncovered an ongoing, one-on-one relationship between the central nervous system and the autoimmune system, the body's natural defense against disease. The key factor in this pattern appears to be the ability to experience all emotions in a full and open manner. Such feelings as hopelessness or helplessness, as well as the inability to express anger, seem to be pertinent factors in suppressing the immune system. Apparently, the feeling messages that we communicate consciously or unconsciously instruct the immune system to either function or disengage. The important implication here is that the emotions that underlie our thoughts, beliefs, values, and behaviors are the source of positive or negative messages to a key resource for maintaining bodily health.

Feelings Are The Key To Health

Long before the advent of psychoneuroimmunology, those of us listening to seriously ill individuals observed that emotions played a pivotal role in recovery. People who are able to deeply acknowledge such feelings as rage, grief, and fear are also capable of moving on to experience fully such feelings as love, hope, and forgiveness. The role of emotions is also directly connected to stress-related problems like burnout.

At the onset of a discussion about the importance of feelings, there are two points to emphasize. The first is that there is no basis for the belief that human beings can rid themselves of unwanted emotions by force of will. Quite the contrary. There is a great deal of evidence to support the premise that all feelings are stored permanently as a function of memory.

Short of doing away with sections of our brains, all feelings—including the ones we don't like to be aware of—are an ongoing part of our humanity. We can deny or numb feelings into unconsciousness, and we can distort and deflect emotions, but we cannot make them disappear. Moreover, when we willingly attempt to limit our experience of uncomfortable emotions, we also limit our experience of the feelings we like. It is a psychological rule of thumb that the highs we experience are directly proportional to the lows we are able to tolerate. In order to experience intense love, peacefulness, and happiness, we must be willing to experience intense sadness, disappointment, and anger. To limit one side of the emotional equation is to automatically limit the other.

Finally, while we cannot effectively rid ourselves of feelings, we are singularly in charge of them. Unlike heredity, the environment, and social factors over which we have relatively little or no direct control, our feelings belong to us. They are ours, and we alone will consciously or unconsciously engage in feeling processes that support or undermine our health.

We Can't Blame Ourselves For The Past

Most adults numb, intellectualize, or dump intensely distressing emotions for reasons that were at one time sound and may even have been life preserving. Yet, what is functional in one context can easily become dysfunctional in another. Chapter 2, "Learning to Feel . . . Again," will elaborate more fully on the logic behind having chosen to block emotions in the past. Unfortunately, when circumstances lead to emotional shutdown, intense feelings are rarely brought back to consciousness under normal circumstances.

Emotional restoration, if or when it takes place, is usually initiated by some kind of a personal or health crisis. Since most of us are unaccustomed to emotional intensity, we do our best to avoid it. To accomplish this end, we have created the most elaborate and ingenious methods for escaping feelings like rage, grief, and fear. Indeed, the avoidance of emotions is a critical factor in bringing about physical disease and is probably the source of all nonorganic psychological distress as well.

A consequence of being afraid to experience certain emotions is that we dare not focus too intensely on any physical or emotional sensation. To do so invites a bubbling up of "frightening feelings" to the surface of consciousness. The process of internal physical focus, for whatever reason, will predictably recall emotions we have avoided experiencing in the past. From this perspective, it is apparent that emotions frequently labeled "unconscious" are simply feelings that we have stored in our bodies and have been able to forget about by focusing our attention elsewhere.

The habit of blocking emotions begins in childhood when feelings are experienced as overpowering and dangerous. Children are overwhelmed by their feelings because they lack experience and the intellectual balance provided by a fully developed cerebral cortex. Moreover, because children lack freedom of choice and are dependent, their options for responding to devastating feelings are grossly limited. They can't fight back or fully absorb the fact that they may not be loved—to do so could be to die.

This, however, is not the case with adults. We are developed intellectually, and freedom is an option whether we recognize it or not. As adults, we have the full range of abilities needed to cope appropriately with any and all of our emotions. The resources for a healthy, life-affirming response to our feelings are within our grasp.

Fear Limits Our Ability To Be Aware Of Our Bodies

Fear prompts us to disconnect from overwhelming emotions and then keeps us locked into patterns of "emotional silencing." Both our feelings and the options we have for doing something constructive about them stay hidden or distorted. In addition, by turning our emotional perceptions down or off, we limit the relationship that we have with our physical bodies. With the exception of a headache, most feelings are experienced somewhere below the bridge of the nose. All emotions have a physical-body-based component and thus produce felt experiences within our bodies. When emotions are lost to consciousness, this "felt sense" of physical sensation is also lost.

As a result, communication with and about our body is obscured, and our lifeline to health is constricted. Further, life-giving energy is trapped and held within the body as a result of emotional blocking. We have to squeeze parts of our bodies and hold them rigid in order to numb, block, or even distort intense feelings. Over time, this holding process absorbs more and more energy.

The process of health requires us to be able to experience a full range of physical and emotional sensations. Note that I am not advocating a disconnection with mental capabilities. We all need to think as well as feel. The problem lies in the fact that while most adults enjoy at least some relationship with their thoughts, they commonly have a very poor relationship with their feelings. This book and the LIVING BEYOND FEAR process that it introduces is intended to be a guide for rediscovering emotional and physical feelings and for reconnecting our minds with our bodies. The LIVING BEYOND FEAR process is a gateway for adding the wisdom of our bodies to our intellectual capabilities in a dependably safe and appropriate manner. The process itself will be introduced in Chapter 7, "Ride the Wild Horse." All the exercises offered up to that point are preparing you for using the process by helping you build your emotional muscles.

Feelings Provide A Barometer For Well-Being

The ability to discern what is going on in our bodies is directly related to our capacity to experience a full range of physical and emotional sensations. Typically, emotional sensations are the first to capture our attention unless we're in pain. Once the emotional charge no longer exists, we can identify physical sensations that guide us toward well-being. How do we distinguish one program or course of treatment from another? We do this by attuning to the subtle feeling sensations in our bodies. Programs and treatments that lead us toward health will be energizing, though they may be difficult to experience. Aggressive treatments will, of course, produce fatigue and can cause discomfort, but, when they are working, a subtle increase in energy can be experienced within a relatively short period of time.

There is more to be discovered in the process of reconnecting with the feeling sensations in our bodies than just raw emotions and bodily awareness. Though blocked emotions are generally the first things we encounter when we begin the process, emotional and bodily awareness is only the beginning. Like oil on the surface of a deep and clear body of water, our difficult, unacceptable feelings cloud our ability to perceive the depths that hold the potential for revival, renewal, and even survival against all odds. We can be sure that an abundance of love, hope, and peace await a willingness to penetrate the unappealing surface layers of emotion. However, beneath the surface awaits something even more amazing, something subtle and yet so profound that in the future it may come to be acknowledged as a source of extraordinary healing capabilities.

QUIZZES AND EXERCISES MAKE THE LIVING BEYOND FEAR PROCESS MORE MEANINGFUL

As mind and body reinforce one another, clarity and understanding grow, and we are able to effect deeper and deeper releases. The emotions and energy liberated by the LIVING BEYOND FEAR process feed back to us via the inventories and exercises for improving perception and awareness. These added insights, in turn, reinforce one's commitment to the process. I suggest that you keep a notebook or diary of your responses to the inventories and exercises, adding drawings and relevant materials if you like.

When it comes to making the best possible use of the time you spend doing the inventories and exercises, there are two rules to follow: (1) observe your feelings, both emotional and physical; and (2) do not judge or criticize any of them. There are no right or wrong answers. The information that you collect is only a guide to your present feelings, thoughts, and behavior. Only by being truthful about the present can we become more constructive in the future.

Simply watch and note your feelings as an interested but involved bystander as you say, "I feel angry." "I feel very sad." "I feel _____." Note how these feelings physically manifest themselves for you—where do you feel them as tension or discomfort in your body? If you find yourself criticizing—"Ugh, I'll never get it right." "How stupid of me." or "What a jerk I am."—notice that also. Keep observing and letting go; observing and letting go. If you find you cannot let go, notice that, too.

I would like to stress that observing your behavior does not mean examining every nuance of feeling you experience. The LBF process is not meant to become an all-consuming 24-hour-a-day exercise in self-involvement. If, however, you confront areas in your life that cause powerful reactions physically and/or emotionally—any behavior that creates real discomfort for you—this is the place to look. I will explain in greater detail later on how to work with these feelings. You may also wish to deal with your reactions as they arise. The process is similar. Simply take note, acknowledge them, and go on about your business. You are learning about yourself. You may not like or even approve of what you notice, but your job is not to judge, just to do the research.

EXPERIENCE THIS BOOK, DON'T JUST READ IT

Learning is a whole-person process, one that must engage and include memory, experience, and physical activity, as well as comprehension.

A cognitive understanding of the concepts in this book is helpful, of course, but it will not create change. However, when theory is taken to the level of action and internalized, real learning occurs. It is much like the difference between reading about the aroma, flavor, and texture of a fresh strawberry and trying one; you really cannot know what it tastes like until you actually eat one. As this book is intended to be experienced, not just read, the exercises are here to help you actively assimilate and integrate self-awareness.

The quizzes and inventories are included to assist you in getting in touch with your attitudes and belief systems. They are not tests. There are no right or wrong answers. There is no passing or failing. Your responses are to be viewed merely as neutral information concerning your perceptions of yourself at this time.

When taking the quizzes, give yourself permission to answer each question truthfully. Sounds preposterous, doesn't it? Why in the world wouldn't you answer them honestly? Don't forget that for many years you may have been denying much of the truth about who you are in order to feel accepted and good about yourself. Answer the questions in the spirit of self-discovery and ignore the internal critic. Begin at the beginning; know yourself.

FREEZE!

Begin where you are this instant. Exactly how do you feel . . . can you tell me? What criteria do you use? Can you check your body, your stomach, or chest for gut reactions, or do you ask your mind to answer the following question, "How am I doing?" Go ahead—check it out. If you haven't already done so, observe exactly how you feel this instant, and hold onto an awareness of the feeling for a few seconds.

Did you surprise yourself at all? Most of the time people don't really pay careful attention to exactly how they're feeling, unless of course they're feeling very bad. In fact, many define feeling good as the absence of feeling bad. How about you?

CREATING A PERSONAL ENERGY SCANNER

Energy is a basic and essential part of life. It takes some energy to do anything, and it takes a little more to begin to do things differently. That's why beginning a new project at the end of the day—or the beginning of the day if you're a night person—is usually a bust! It's much easier to begin and keep going when you start during that time of day when you normally feel the most energized.

Most of us first become aware of energy as a sensation of liveliness, excitement, or well-being contained within our physical bodies. It's very apparent, for example, when you have just completed an invigorating run or swim, or the minute you receive very good news, that you feel uplifted. Listening to your favorite piece of music can do the same thing for you as being with someone you love very much. It's as if everything becomes clearer, lighter—there is more joy to life. Energy is also defined by some as get-up-and-go or enthusiasm. It is all these and much, much more.

1. Imagine you are a radar-like energy scanner that periodically appraises what you are doing and how you feel doing it. The scanner will stop and take into account your sense of feeling uplifted or being brought down by a situation, person, or event. For example, you just had lunch with your best friend. Do you feel uplifted or deflated by the experience? Take another situation—a family gathering—what's your awareness now? Did the scanner register a gain or loss in terms of the energy generated by the experience? Chances are that if you pay careful attention, you will experience energy shifts as you move from situation to situation during the day that cannot be explained away by hunger or fatigue.

2. You may wish to write your observations down or chart them with the following headings: "What Am I Doing?" "How Do I Feel Doing What I'm Doing?" "How Is My Energy Being Affected?" Continue to make notations until the process becomes habitual.

3. Stay in the "witness state." Remember that your ability to attune energetically is related to the objectivity of your scanning device. You will begin to observe much more in terms of how your energy lifts or diminishes if you maintain a neutral but interested posture.

OBSERVING THE DIFFERENCE BETWEEN GOALS AND PROCESSES

Self-awareness is tied to the ability to discern internal processes. This exercise is intended to enhance this awareness.

1. Before you go to bed at night, or when you get up in the morning, make a plan for the day from the point of the objectives you wish to accomplish. For example, you may plan to exercise from 7:00 to 7:30; breakfast at 8:00; work beginning at 9:30 a.m.; complete letters; calls by lunch time; Lunch with X; meeting from 2:00 to 4:00 p.m.; meditate from 6:00 to 7:00 p.m.; etc. . . . This plan will of course vary greatly depending on your circumstances, but even if you are ill you can organize your day in segments that focus on specific goals. Do this for a few days, noting the quality of your life as you pay attention in this manner.

2. After you have focused for a few days, shift your attention from the accomplishment of tasks to that of experiencing what takes place in between the times when your objectives are being accomplished. What is the quality of life like for you then? What does it feel like to be between objectives? What does it feel like to be accomplishing "nothing in particular?" People ask, "Is one mode better than the other?" The answer is that both are necessary and important parts of a full and balanced life.

DAILY GOALS/DAILY PROCESSES

Time	Objectives	Process	Comments
7 A.M.	Exercise/ stationary bike.	Laborious.	Not much fun.
8:00	Dress/breakfast.	Hurrying.	Rushed.
9:30	Work/check phone messages.	"	Too many calls.
10:30 to 11:00	Staff meeting.	Irritating/ competitive.	It's all a blur.
12:00 to 1 P.M.	Lunch w. friend.	Fun.	Stimulating conversation.
2:00	Meeting w. X.	Sleepy.	Looking at clock.
3:00	Meeting w. Y.	Dull.	"
4:00	Meeting w. Z.	Dull.	"
5:00	Paperwork/calls.	Hurrying to get out.	Feel focused and intense.
6:00	Commute home.	Heavy traffic, angry, frustrated.	
7:00	Dinner.	Exhausted/ empty.	
8:00	Watch news.	Interesting.	
9:00	Read.	Enjoyable.	
10:00	To bed.		Not much fun!

CHAPTER 2

Learning to Feel . . . Again

> *"We should not pretend to understand the world only by intellect; we apprehend it just as much by feeling."*
>
> —Carl Jung

At a family reunion, I was surprised and delighted—but deeply shocked—to run into a cousin I had idealized, but not seen since childhood. I could barely contain my sadness as I listened to him describe in stoic detail his chronic ailments and unhappy life. Was this the same rowdy cousin who had swept the rest of us along on his exciting adventures? Was this the same fellow who had kept us in rapt attention with his zany antics and zest for life? Where had his spirit, his vitality, his feeling Self, gone?

HOW FEELINGS GET LOST AND STAY LOST: EMOTIONAL SHUTDOWN

A natural and necessary part of ''growing up'' is separating from the dominating influence of raw feeling, such as striking out when we do not get our way or screaming in fury when we are told, "No!" Obviously, it is necessary early in life to learn to postpone or even to deny gratification, or to limit emotional expression. There are times when doing or saying exactly what we wish would be totally inappropriate. In our culture, throwing food across the room when we do not like what has been served, going to the bathroom anywhere and anytime we please, assaulting people as the mood strikes us, are all grounds for immediate ostracization.

Four-year-old Amy learned that she could not always say indiscriminately what she pleased. During a cocktail party her parents were hosting one evening, Amy walked into the living room and announced to her mother in her normally loud child's voice, "Mommy, my vagina burns." The room responded with a mixture of stunned silence and snickers. Her embarrassed mother whisked her off to explain a few of the unwritten rules of self-expression.

Growing up often is emotionally painful. We learn very early through parents, siblings, and relatives that others are not always in agreement with our feelings and desires. Because our safety as young children is connected to others, and since our feelings and instincts are often in direct disagreement, this socialization process is frequently frustrating and stressful.

A child's natural reaction to denied wants, pain, fear, and frustration is tears and tantrums. These responses are usually met with, "Stop crying." "Knock it off." "Go to your room." "If you don't stop crying, I'm really going to give you something to cry about." a spanking, or the most devastating approach of all, the "silent treatment." Few parents feel comfortable when a child is hurt and cries, especially if they feel responsible. Their reaction is to stop the tears, the display of emotion. As a child, all one understands is that one's natural responses have brought rejection. Out of our fear of continued disapproval or withdrawn affection, the child learns to deny spontaneity, repress the hurt that caused the tears, and, ultimately, learns to separate from his or her feelings—just as our parents did before us.

When two-and-a-half-year-old Michael was told emphatically that he could not play in Daddy's tackle box, he began to scream and cry his displeasure. After all, Daddy was playing in it; why couldn't he? Daddy, on the other hand, felt guilty about making his son cry, so he angrily yelled, "Shut up or I'll send you to your room!" Michael had a choice—to continue to express his hurt and be exiled to his room or to swallow his feelings and stay with Daddy.

Some choice. Michael stayed, of course, but he had to do something to alleviate the stress, so he forced his feelings inward. He breathed rapidly and shallowly. He tensed his face, neck, and upper back; his diaphragm froze, his stomach knotted as his digestive system shut down from throat to anus; and he cut off the tears. Eventually, the painful feelings subsided, he breathed normally, and, due to the mercifully short attention span of children, he was distracted elsewhere. But an automatic response was beginning to be formed; Michael was learning to disconnect from his emotions. He learned how to protect himself from emotional pain, but he would pay a lifelong price for that protection.

Most of us are like Amy and Michael. We have developed habits and responses that often eliminate our capacity to relate to ourselves or others. We master the art of denying our feelings. We look at our watches to see if we are hungry or tired. We take pills to elevate or depress our moods and appetites; to make us tired; to wake us up; to

LEARNING TO FEEL . . . AGAIN

shut out the vaguest pain or ache. We go through the social motions of meeting new people but rarely make any real contact. We blink back tears even in a dark theater; chuckle uncomfortably during painfully emotional good-byes; fake orgasms; brush off compliments; laugh nervously at unfunny jokes; avoid eye contact; and seldom say what we honestly feel. And the list goes on.

Not only do we wish to avoid uncomfortable feelings, but we live in a state of semiconsciousness during emotional highs as well. We resist being "carried away" by the crescendo of exquisite music or the overwhelming excitement of the vastness and beauty of nature. We are frightened off by the depth and intimacy possible in an emotional conversation with a dear friend or by the power and sensuality of sex with someone we deeply love. We negate acknowledgment for personal achievements and restrict our pleasure and excitement even in our greatest victories. Do you remember the last time you literally jumped for joy or whooped and cried in surprise and elation? We never seem to go all the way; there is always a holdback.

By the time Amy, Michael, and the rest of us are school age, we have a set of memories and expectations that will accompany us out into the world. At six, seven, or eight, we actually have far more self-control than we did as toddlers, but we may not be aware of this fact. We may have become so accustomed to protecting ourselves and shutting down emotionally that we turn off automatically. Sooner or later, this emotional shutdown will hurt us socially and intellectually. Our creativity, learning, and social development will be inhibited, and the impression we make on others may be that we are dumb, disinterested, preoccupied, self-centered, antisocial, stuck up, etc.

Moreover, once a pattern is set, our expectations of hurt and rejection may contribute to obnoxious behavior that insures the rejection we fear.

At puberty, the expectations and emotional habits we have formulated will carry over into our intimate relationships. Further, since emotional shutdown is common in our society, we will most likely be involved with individuals who also numb and disguise their feelings. When this is the case and both individuals are disconnected from their feelings, it is likely that they will also disconnect from each other. On the positive side, however, close relationships trigger memories that help us reconnect with blocked emotions and this gives us an opportunity to know and process them appropriately.

RELATIONSHIPS TEACH US ABOUT OURSELVES—OUCH!

One can live alone for many years and keep up the illusion of emotional equanimity, but as soon as we let someone become close to us, the bubble pops. Professor Henry Higgins expressed it well in the celebrated musical, "My Fair Lady": "Let a woman [or a man] in your life and you invite eternal strife." Perhaps "eternal strife" is a bit of an exaggeration, but there is no escaping the fact that intimacy stirs us up emotionally. Because this is the case, people with whom we have very close and involving relationships—mates, lovers, parents, siblings, children, some friendships—help us to learn about ourselves.

Intimates, like mirrors, reflect our own behavior, exasperating as this may be. We can begin to recognize a great deal about ourselves by paying attention to the emotional responses of those we care deeply for or where we have a great deal invested in our emotional reactions to these responses.

FEELING AWARENESS ENHANCES SELF-CONTROL

Over and over again adults confuse intensity of feeling with loss of control. The fear is that if we experience the full depth of our feelings, we will be overwhelmed by them. This is just not so, but the key word here is *experience*. If feelings are felt as physical sensations in our bodies, they will not overwhelm us—provided we process them appropriately. If we numb them, twist or intellectualize them, we can lose control. The reason any feeling is manageable, if we experience it, is that adults can reason in ways that children cannot, and thus have choices that children do not have. While emotional maturity is reached by age five or six, intellectual maturity—including judgment, is not fully developed until the late teen years. The cerebral cortex (the area of our brain that governs, among other things, judgment) develops more slowly than the part that controls emotional development. Small children occasionally have tantrums that often end in exhausting crying bouts, yet, they never seem to die or go mad from overwhelmingly intense emotions. Adults, on the other hand, guided by judgment, can choose their behavioral responses. Emotion and intellect are able to function simultaneously in mature adults. This has far-reaching implications. It makes it possible to be both full of feeling and fully functional at the same time. In other words, "feeling awareness" can allow us to fully experience sadness or anger, elation or love, while we continue to be productive, creative, and sensitive to others and to our environment.

STRESS RESULTS FROM AVOIDING FEELING

Every emotion, particularly fear and anger, has an immediate and sympathetic response in the body. Our very survival as a species has depended upon it. "Fight or flight" is a prehistoric, an archaic physiological response mechanism that kept us alive, either dashing from saber-toothed tigers or clubbing our enemies. It is an immediate, spontaneous reaction based on actual or perceived life-threatening situations. Anxiety is a term that describes psychologically perceived threats. Stress, the modern equivalent to "fight or flight," is triggered by changes in our lives or things we perceive as threatening. Fighting or running are not acceptable behaviors in a modern world, but the emotions that go hand in glove with the "fight or flight" reflex are triggered in instances of psychological danger as well as physical danger. When we feel threatened but numb, or misplace our physical or emotional responses, the energy that has been triggered remains unresolved. We thus prolong the state of "fight or flight" and this eventually becomes both physically and emotionally undermining.

When your garage mechanic estimates your bill at $650, labor not included, you cannot release your outrage by bouncing your fist off his face (especially if he is bigger than you are). Instead, you internalize your anger, either by swallowing it and remaining coolly passive (though your insides may feel like a churning sea), or by yelling a few obscenities and storming off (which only vents rather than exhausts the anger). Neither behavior resolves the situation. You may spend the rest of the day seething and then go home to verbally or physically abuse the people or pets you live with. You will undoubtedly spend the day reliving your anxiety as you tell and retell the story of your victimization to anyone who will listen. Somehow, though, you will succeed in suppressing your genuine anger and resentful feelings. The toll you will pay for turning off anger is stress.

Migraine headaches, insomnia, chronic fatigue, backaches, ulcers, colitis, hypoglycemia, asthma, high blood pressure, nonspecific dermatitis, arthritis, and a host of other emotion-related physical disorders are examples of ailments brought on by repressed emotions and ignored stresses. Though these disorders in themselves are bad enough, often they are also the precursors of more devastating diseases.

PHYSICAL AWARENESS SUPPORTS EMOTIONAL RECOVERY

As a young woman, I frequently complained to my doctor that I had a feeling in my chest as if a sack of stones were contained there. It was a heavy, constricted feeling that made me fear a potential heart attack. The tension and tightness pulled my whole shoulder girdle forward and made me appear round-shouldered and old. The doctor never could find any evidence of heart trouble though the sack of stones persisted in weighing my chest down.

When as a result of my early experimentations with the LIVING BEYOND FEAR process, I became more sensitive to bodily perceptions and began to relax and open up to my fears. I realized that I was trying to protect my heart from all the sadness I felt, and as I continued to expose my defenses and denials, the "stones" began to disappear and my body resumed its normal posture and contour. Whenever I feel threatened, I can still feel my chest begin to tighten and I start to hunch my shoulders. But now I am able to control my once-automatic response to perceived threat. I process my fear by focusing on feeling sensations in my body—both physical and emotional. No more stones!

The body is a teacher, a great storehouse of physical, emotional, and intuitive information and wisdom that sends subtle but interpretable messages constantly. Every emotional experience has its counterpart in the body. When these feelings are blocked or repressed, the emotional memories are locked in at muscular and visceral levels, but we can use our bodies to provide the way back to rediscovering our emotions. We can relearn to feel how we feel, not just think how we feel. Any sensation, therefore, that brings attention to our physical selves is a valuable clue to our emotional selves as well.

PHYSICAL FITNESS SUPPORTS EMOTIONAL FITNESS

Physical fitness techniques help us become more aware of our bodies. This is especially true if in the process of exercising we pay attention to the bodily sensations that we feel. Exercise is appropriate for everyone, including those who are seriously ill, provided it is gentle. Tai Chi or Yoga have been found to be beneficial to individuals on chemotherapy. Walking, swimming, and low-impact aerobics not only tone and strengthen our bodies but can trigger the release of endorphins—substances in the brain that inspire us and raise our spirits. Individuals find that exercise is an excellent way to prepare themselves for practicing the LIVING BEYOND FEAR process presented in Chapter Seven.

The more physically sensitive we become, the more whole and vital we will feel.

As you progress through the chapters, a great many sensitive areas will be uncovered. If you are like most people, you will do almost anything to escape feeling emotionally unsettled or uncomfortable. You may numb your feelings by distracting yourself with almost anything, including your obsessive-compulsive thoughts. You may want to eat, sleep, watch TV, smoke, work, focus on taking care of others, etc. You may want to create a distracting personal drama or get rid of your emotions by dumping them on someone else. But the very act of avoiding pain dulls everything else that is useful, positive, constructive, healthy, and life-affirming. Practice the LIVING BEYOND FEAR process and hold onto the intention to physically experience your feelings.

FEELING AWARENESS QUIZZES

Remember, nothing is right or wrong, good or bad; all is useful information. Answer each question rapidly, without giving it thought, no matter how surprising your response may be.

THE PART FEELINGS PLAY IN MY LIFE

*Fill in the letter code of the word that best applies:
N = Never, R = Rarely, S = Sometimes, F = Frequently,
A = Always.*

1. I _____ can tell by the way that I feel when I'm about to get a cold or get sick.

2. I ____ experience a full range of feeling in my day-to-day existence, including sadness, anger, and fear.

3. Breathing deeply ____ makes me feel uncomfortable.

4. My intense emotions ____ cause me to feel "out of control."

5. Other people's intense emotions ____ cause me to feel out of control.

6. I ____ am aware of my energy level.

7. I am ____ aware of parts of my body that feel tense.

8. When I'm tired I ____ drink coffee, etc., to keep going.

9. I am ____ moved by other people's feelings.

10. I ____ cry.

11. I ____ laugh.

12. I ____ get angry.

13. I ____ feel really high (naturally).

14. I ____ feel frightened.

15. I ____ like attuning to physical sensations.

16. I ____ enjoy stretching and moving my body.

17. When I was a kid I ____ experienced intense emotions.

18. Physical/emotional perceptions are ____ a part of my awareness.

THE NATURE OF MY FEELINGS

1. What, if any, are the ways in which you care for your physical body? List at least five if you can.

2. Do you consider sexuality to be connected to your physical well-being, and if so what do you do to care for yourself sexually?

3. Are you aware of the role that food plays in terms of

your physical/emotional well-being? If so, what do you do to ensure your ongoing state of health.

4. Are you aware of the role that exercise plays in terms of your physical/emotional well-being? If so, what do you consistently do to maintain your ongoing state of health?

5. Have you changed in terms of feeling awareness since childhood?

HOW DOES PHYSICAL AND EMOTIONAL EXPERIENCE SHAPE MY LIFE?

The following self-evaluation quiz will help you determine your present level of physical and emotional awareness. Treat this quiz as you would a research project on yourself. Nothing is right or wrong, good or bad; all is useful information. Answer each question rapidly without giving it any thought, no matter how silly or surprising your responses may be. Review your answers after finishing this chapter, and note whether or not they now reveal more to you.

Circle the answer that best describes how you feel.

1. I like touching and being touched.   T   F
2. It embarrasses me to have anyone see   T   F
   me cry.
3. My feelings get hurt easily.   T   F
4. Sex is often very pleasurable for me.   T   F
5. When someone compliments me, I get   T   F
   embarrassed.
6. I feel edgy without a drink at social gath-   T   F
   erings.

7. I'm able to listen when someone is angry   T   F
with me.
8. There are parts of my body that are never   T   F
relaxed.
9. Anger does not intimidate me.   T   F
10. Emotions seem to run my life.   T   F
11. I feel tense much of the time.   T   F
12. It is easy for me to express my feelings.   T   F
13. I don't like intense feelings.   T   F
14. I don't like strangers to touch me.   T   F
15. I rarely get emotional.   T   F
16. I pay attention to how my body feels.   T   F
17. I show affection freely.   T   F

WHERE DO I FEEL THE FEELINGS?

Write down your initial response to the following questions, using only one or two words.

1. When I'm angry, I feel it in my _____.
2. When I feel sad, I feel it in my _____.
3. Tension registers itself most frequently in my

    _____.
4. When I feel tense, I _____.
5. My favorite form of exercise is _____.
6. Masturbation is _____.
7. I often feel pain in my _____.
8. When my mate sees me nude, I feel _____.
9. Fear makes me feel like _____.
10. When I see someone crying, I feel _____.
11. I'm happiest when I'm _____.
12. Arguments make me feel _____.
13. I feel most out of control when I'm _____.

14. Nothing frightens me more than _____.
15. The last time I really felt vital and alive was _____.

INVENTORY FOR TURNING FEAR INTO INTIMACY

The following are some of the more common fears associated with intimacy: Do you identify with any of these? Which one or ones? How does your behavior reflect your fear?

1. Fear of losing oneself—of giving up personal identity in exchange for being loved.
2. Fear of not being lovable, acceptable, or good—or good enough.
3. Fear of loss of control, not being in charge of myself and/or my life.
4. Fear of rejection and abandonment, of not being liked, accepted, or loved.

Whatever we're afraid of, two things are likely to be true: First, fear is not likely to be expressed directly as fear, but rather through manipulating and controlling behaviors toward ourselves and others. Secondly, the patterns of fear—manipulation and control—arose as the result of the interaction we perceived with our parents in early childhood. The way we related with intimates then is the way we're apt to relate today.

1. The next time you feel more than momentarily upset with someone important to you, ask the following

questions: "What part or parts of my body are tense, tight, or heavy in this moment of distress?"

2. "Do I feel the feelings that I associate with fear?" If the answer from your body is in any way "Yes," then continue by asking, "What am I afraid of?" Possibilities might include rejection, abandonment, feelings of inadequacy, loss of control, loss of self.

3. Tune into the physical feelings and ask, "When in the past do I remember feeling this way?" Let the memories progressively take you back to earlier and earlier periods of your life.

EXTENDING MY RANGE OF FEELING AWARENESS

Fill in the letter code of the word that best applies: N = Never, R = Rarely, S = Sometimes, F = Frequently, A = Always.

1. I ____ feel good about my sexual identity.
2. I am ____ happy to be who I am.
3. My life ____ feels meaningful.
4. Sex is ____ fun.
5. I am ____ satisfied with the choices I have made.
6. When I'm with a man, I'm ____ comfortable.
7. When I'm with a woman, I'm ____ comfortable.
8. I ____ enjoy or have enjoyed anonymous sex.
9. I ____ use sex now or have used sex as a distraction when I'm bored or unhappy.
10. I ____ feel good about my body.
11. I ____ feel that options are available to me.
12. I ____ feel good about my mother.
13. I ____ feel good about my father.

14. I ____ feel lovable.
15. I ____ feel good about most people.
16. I ____ feel good about most sick people.
17. I ____ feel that I have something worthwhile to contribute to life.
18. I ____ feel that disease is a punishment for being bad.

FEELING EXERCISES

The following exercises are designed to help you dynamically explore many of the emotions you have suppressed over the years. As emotions and feelings surface for you, simply be aware of them without judging or criticizing them. ("I'm scared." "I'm frustrated." "I'm peaceful.") Notice whether you are open to or protected from these feelings. Notice your emotions as they relate to your bodily sensations. Where do you feel stuck or defensive? Be aware of your posture, breathing, muscular tensions, or aches and pains as indicators of areas that need further exploration. Above all, be patient with and kind to yourself. The more aware you become, even when that means feeling uncomfortable, the more in charge you will feel and be in your life.

BREATHING LIFE INTO FEELING

Set aside thirty minutes of your hour for this exercise. Before you begin, make an agreement with yourself that you will move on to your other activities at the end of the hour. You will begin to prove to yourself that experiencing strong emotions will not keep you from your usual productivity. In fact, getting on with your life, even though feeling deeply, is the best way to free yourself of the fear you may have about intensely experiencing emotions.

Lie down or sit comfortably, and loosen restrictive clothing. Begin by turning your attention to your breathing. Inhale slowly, inflating both your chest and belly in any order that feels comfortable to you. Then exhale, making sure to expel all of the breath you inhaled. After ten complete breaths, continue to breathe slowly and rhythmically, visualizing your breath moving throughout the different parts of your body. Starting at the toes and moving slowly upward, inhale into each body part. As you exhale, tell each part to melt and surrender any tensions that may be housed there. Feet . . . calves . . . thighs . . . pelvis . . . lower back . . . stomach . . . internal organs . . . chest . . . lungs . . . heart . . . upper back . . . fingers . . . hands . . . lower arms . . . upper arms . . . shoulders . . . neck . . . head . . . face.

Remember to exhale completely and to continue the slow, deep breathing as you focus on how these various parts of your body feel physically and emotionally. As you continue this breathing exercise, it is not uncommon for intense emotions—emotions that have been stored in your musculature for a very long time—to surface. Allow these feelings to penetrate your awareness.

SCANNING FOR FEELING

This is a very short but highly effective exercise that will support you in your intention to stay open to your feelings. Several times during the day, quickly scan your body and locate the area that seems to house the most feeling. Take a deep breath, focusing on the area, and as you exhale, soften around the center of the feeling.

Repeat with one or two more breaths. Simply acknowledge whatever emotion comes up for you ("That feels angry." or "I feel such joy."). Notice your happiness, too! Do not try to push any emotions away; just feel and take note of them.

You may wish to key into this exercise by agreeing with yourself that every time you get in your car or pick up your house keys or brush your teeth—whatever activity you think will serve best to remind you—you will repeat the exercise.

MOVING TO MUSIC

Put on something comfortable or, if you wish, wear nothing. Clear the floor, shut the door, take the phone off the hook, and select a piece of music that moves and excites you. As the music starts, pretend you are a rock star, folk dancer, ballerina, tribal dancer, bird, chorus boy—whatever your imagination produces.

Begin by moving slowly at first until you warm up. As you feel more relaxed, move in random ways—sitting, lying down, standing, kneeling. Try stretching, shuffling, jumping, kicking, hopping, spinning. Try different qualities of movement. For instance, move slowly, as though you were under water. Try moving jerkily; then rapidly. Try any and every type of movement you can think of to experience every part of your body and the full range of its motion. Play with the idea of moving in as many different ways as you can.

BLINDFOLD EXERCISE

You will need a scarf or handkerchief large enough to serve as a blindfold. Choose a room you are familiar with and comfortable in, as you are going to be exploring it sightlessly. Again, arrange not to be disturbed. Pick an area of the room where you would like to begin the exercise. You are going to begin by slowly and easily feeling your way around the room, letting your other senses expand.

Run your hands over familiar objects, listen to the sounds you make as you move through the room, perhaps picking up different items to examine by touch, taste, and feel. Notice how you feel emotionally and physically as you explore your environment in a much more physical way than you usually do. In what ways are your judgments and perceptions about what has become so familiar to your life different?

Now tie your blindfold in place and get to know more about your world and your feelings.

Note: If you feel frightened about moving around while blindfolded, you may do a variation of this exercise: Choose a table or countertop that has several familiar objects on it. Either sit or stand before it, blindfold yourself, and examine the surface of the table, the objects, etc., as above. Later, as you build more confidence, you may wish to try this exercise as originally suggested.

S-T-R-E-T-C-H

Stretching is a particularly easy, convenient, and awareness-enhancing form of physical movement that tones, invigorates, and stimulates our bodies. It also has the added benefit of causing us to breathe deeply and fully. Animals and children are our teachers here; they stretch constantly. Movement also stimulates mental processes—stretching often, especially when you have been seated and concentrating for long periods, will enhance creativity and productivity.

So resolve to stretch frequently and breathe deeply throughout your day. To help yourself keep this resolution, visualize pleasurable stretching movements before you fall asleep at night and when you awaken in the morning. Simply engage three or more of your five senses—sight, touch, sound, smell, and taste—as you visualize yourself stretching, breathing, yawning.

FOCUS ON SENSUAL FEELING

1. Focus on a sexual experience that was difficult for you. Pay attention to where the feelings are in your body. Breathe into that area and allow yourself to acknowledge and clear your feelings about it.
2. Focus on a sexual experience that was good for you; pay attention to where the feelings are in your body. Breathe into that area and allow the good feelings to expand until your entire body is flooded with them.
3. Standing or sitting in front of a mirror, do an inventory of each part of your body, starting at the toes, and working upward. Do this exercise nude if you

can, or begin with clothes on if nudity is uncomfortable, and do the exercise a few times before trying it in the nude. As you focus on each part of your body, remain uncritical. See each part as having a function and accept it as part of the wholeness of you. If there are parts that are not completely functional, become aware of how that has caused you to move your focus somewhere else, to learn something new. Feel the feelings in each part as you inventory it, and simply let whatever feelings are there be there—accept them as a part of the larger whole. They may change as you do this, and if the feelings change, accept the changes also. (This exercise may require several repetitions over a period of time before you are comfortable with it.)

4. Using the sense of wholeness—of many parts working in concert to create a body that is more than the total of all its parts—picture your whole self as a mysterious and beautiful system, working in ways you may not understand, to be healthy and efficient. Appreciate the smoothness of this system and breathe into those parts that are out of rhythm; feel the pulse of that rhythm grow smoother and stronger.

SOUND OFF!

Here you get to play with sound and your anxiety level in expressing it. You may feel a bit uncomfortable at first; our Western culture does little to facilitate our communicating feeling in ways other than polite conversation or an occasional "rah-rah" at a ballgame.

There are three places you may wish to try out this exercise before you feel comfortable enough to attempt it within earshot of others: in your room with the radio or stereo turned up loud enough to drown you out; driving in your car with the windows rolled up; or in the shower with the bathroom door shut. But do not be concerned. Pretty soon your friends and family will ignore your strange behavior.

Find your place and begin experimenting with your sounds: shout; laugh; make sounds from high in the throat, i.e., *eeeeeeeh*, or as deep as possible in the body, like *uuggghh*, *wuuuff*; grunt or groan; sing; try nonsense sounds, like *mumumumumum*, *bobobobobobobo*; make baby noises; stick your tongue out and blow a raspberry; make faces. Sound off!

Notice how you feel physically and emotionally as you make these sounds. Anxious? Tense? Happy? Do you bellow them out, or meow? Do you sound like a lusty animal or a bird whistle? Feel how much or how little you are holding back, and reflect on how that reflects itself in your life.

INVENTORY FOR PARTNERS OF MEN AND WOMEN WITH LIFE-THREATENING ILLNESS

Remember, nothing is right or wrong, good or bad; all is useful information. Answer each question rapidly without giving it any thought, no matter how surprising your response may be. If a response troubles you, review the chapter in the book that relates to the feeling.

FEELINGS ABOUT MY MATE

Fill in the letter code of the word that best applies:
N = Never, R = Rarely, S = Sometimes, F = Frequently,
A = Always.

1. I ___ feel tenderness for my partner.
2. I ___ feel sexually attracted to my partner.
3. I ___ feel angry at my partner.
4. I ___ feel emotionally close to my partner.
5. I ___ feel betrayed by my partner.
6. I ___ feel compassion for my partner.
7. I ___ feel victimized by my partner.
8. I ___ feel like running away from my partner.
9. I ___ feel that I don't have the strength to continue supporting my partner.
10. I ___ feel frightened by my partner's illness.
11. I ___ feel ashamed of my feelings.
12. I ___ feel that I should be more loving toward my partner.
13. I ___ feel that I should be more supportive of my partner.
14. I ___ feel afraid of being infected by my partner.
15. I ___ feel that I have failed my partner in some way.
16. I ___ wish that my partner would die.
17. I ___ feel like a good person.
18. I ___ feel like a bad person.
19. I ___ feel like asking for help.
20. I ___ feel that it is okay for me to accept love and support at this time.

PART II

Opening

CHAPTER 3

Criticism, Judgment, and Punishment

*"It is only with the heart that one can see rightly;
what is essential is invisible to the eye."*
—Antoine de Saint Exupéry

A number of years ago, I bought one of those inexpensive scorekeepers that golfers use and carried it around with me for a day. Each time I had a critical or judgmental thought, I clicked the button. By the end of the day, I estimated that I had clicked off perhaps a dozen putdowns—but my score was actually fifty-three!

The voice of judgment is indiscriminate, insular, biased, and crippling. It serves as a protective cover for disowned feelings of rage, sadness, despair, and fear. For example:

> I'm no good.
> My sister is a witch.
> My father is cold and unfeeling.
> She cares only about herself.

He thinks only about his business.
I can't do anything right.

Criticism is a voice we direct toward ourselves: I'm a bad kid, student, lover, athlete, provider, mother. I'm always acting like a fool, a slob, eating too much, on the make. Criticism is also a weapon we direct at others: You're never affectionate, happy, dependable, appreciative, here when I need you. You are so inconsiderate, thoughtless, unfeeling. You should call your mother more often, go to church, clean up the house, look more attractive, dress better, pay attention, become more political, be more spiritual. He's/She's too fat, thin, tall, slow, emotional, sloppy, sweaty, hairy, round-shouldered, cheap, unimaginative, successful, sexy, lazy, and much too demanding. They are disgusting, unnatural, sick, stupid, dishonest, and evil.

The list is long and ludicrous but deadly realistic nonetheless. According to the voices of criticism within and without we cannot possibly ever be good enough physically, emotionally, intellectually, or spiritually, and that just about covers the range of human possibilities.

Not all criticism is emotionally inspired and not all punishment inappropriate. Limit-setting is an essential part of civilized life, as is discernment. Looking at the world through rose-colored glasses is no healthier, more appropriate, or realistic than viewing it as a dung heap. The point is to be able to differentiate between discerning, critical evaluation based on intellectual maturity, and criticism based on disowned feelings.

CRITICAL THOUGHTS PROTECT EMOTIONAL VULNERABILITIES

Criticism, judgment, and punishment occur at thinking, feeling, and behavioral levels. To understand the role that criticism plays in our lives, we have to carefully attune to the emotional charge coming through at the feeling level. Are we angry, hurt, or frightened? Do emotions motivate judgmental thoughts and punishing actions? Are we once again "thinking our feelings," creating reasons to be critical in order to protect emotional vulnerability. Are we reflexively repeating old emotionally charged patterns that no longer apply or are helpful?

Another way to appraise critical, judgmental, and punitive behavior is to question the intent behind the statement or action. Is there an emotional charge mixed into the process? Are we obsessing? Are we acting one way but feeling another? Are we trying to be rational, reasonable, and objective while seething inside, or feeling very vulnerable? When we are full of feeling—so full that all our energy is going into pushing the emotions away—we are simply not going to be able to listen. First we have to focus on the charged feelings and how easy it is to avoid such feelings by distracting ourselves with obsessive critical thoughts.

JUDGMENT AND CRITICISM DISTORT REALITY

Judgment and criticism are no-win games, yet, to some extent, we all play just the same. It feels so natural. Our parents, our teachers, and the media modeled and assessed our values and set our moral polarities of good and bad, right and wrong. "Be a good boy, Tommy." "You're such a naughty little girl, Nancy." One is as narrow and limiting as the other. It matters little what you were actually doing—you could have been clubbing your brother or tracking mud on the carpet. Every action received a moral judgment, and it did not take long before this value system was internalized. As adults we continue to evaluate every possible thought, feeling, and behavior morally and simplistically. The consequences are two-fold: Morality loses its valid life-giving connection; and anything less than "all good" becomes "all bad." The former results in amorality, the latter in absurdity.

We perceive from a one-dimensional perspective when we are critical of ourselves or others, whether the criticism is verbalized or implied. Can anyone be only one way? Can anyone always be selfish, unfeeling, stingy, dumb, unattractive, judgmental? Or, using the premise that they are—what if they are because of conditioning, fear, or ignorance? Can we really label anyone, ourselves included, for something we are capable of seeing only fractionally? When we think or tell Harry that he's a dummy because he cannot balance his checkbook, and yet he is bilingual, aren't we perceiving only one attribute out of many, and that one irrationally? Who are we kidding? Isn't Harry really just a fellow who has not learned to subtract? But what happens when Harry believes us?

We judge every situation from one point of view—namely, our own—as if it were cosmic truth. It is precisely this absolute, all-inclusive nature of criticism and judgment that distinguishes it from observation and discernment.

When you look at yourself or another and see only one view, you have set aside rational thinking and are riding on emotion. Observation and discernment simultaneously engage both rational thinking and feeling. This allows us to assess the situation mentally as well as feel it. We have the ability to view the whole even as the part is being seen. It is possible to see a messy room as an unsatisfactory job, carelessness, even cruelty, and dislike the situation intensely without passing judgment on the totality of the person who created it (including ourselves). All-inclusive, permanent labels are unneeded and unwarranted. It is quite possible to experience the momentary coolness of a loved one, even feel the hurt, and know there remains a depth of feeling that goes beyond the immediate experience.

An "all bad" or "all good" classification closes the doors to learning change and growth. If we are "all bad," what is the point of even trying; and if we are "all good," who needs to make the effort? Learning is motivated by imperfection, and grounded in the willingness to be a beginner. Our unwillingness to experience vulnerability limits our ability to achieve desired goals. Adults are unwilling to be imperfect beginners. One of the reasons children have an easier time learning than do adults is that children, when unhampered by critical adults, have no preconceived ideas about what excellence is. They are not afraid of failing. They are uninhibited and involved in the process of learning; they do not see themselves as awkward or inept—until someone convinces them they are. They are excited about the discovery of knowledge. The moment is magical, not the end result. Because as adults we seek perfection at each step, self-criticism and judgment inhibit us far more than any lack of ability.

CRITICISM OF OTHERS MASKS
CRITICISM OF SELF

Criticism of others is linked to criticism of ourselves. The line between what we cannot forgive in ourselves and what we are unable to forgive in others is very thin. So often the gut-wrenching responses we have toward others is an indication of disliked and disowned parts of ourselves. Those aspects of our personality that we have judged bad or incomplete, or are afraid or ashamed to recognize, are brought into focus by the unacceptable behaviors of others.

Years ago, during a seminar I was attending, I was puzzled by the intensity of my responses to one of my fellow participants. She was a bright, articulate young woman who repeatedly spoke up and made her views known. I could not find fault with what she said; but to my outwardly disguised horror, I found that every time she opened her mouth I had a terrific desire to put my fist in it. My irritation was so intense I practically had to sit on my hands.

Perceiving this reaction to be extreme, not to mention irrational, I gritted my teeth and attuned to the strong sensations in the pit of my stomach. At first I could only identify anger, but as I sat with my feelings, other stronger emotions surfaced. To my great embarrassment, what surfaced was jealousy. She was getting the attention I wanted, and it irked me. Here was a woman not so different from myself, standing up, speaking out, and receiving appreciation for her ideas, while I, conversely, sat in my chair still as a mouse. It was difficult for me to speak out at that time—I still had a tremendous fear of appearing ignorant or foolish. I was also extremely critical of my need for attention, for to me any kind of need was weakness, and weakness was infantile. Moreover, jealousy was petty, embarrassing, and undignified. I was trapped by my own judgments, and the tightness and pain I felt in my body attested to how much control they exercised.

Our most intensely emotional reactions to judgments and criticism can teach us a great deal about ourselves. The gut-grabbing response to someone or something can reveal in a moment what might take years to dredge up in traditional therapy. This is not to say that there are not some people and situations that we instinctively feel are detrimental to our well-being. These messages are usually clear and should be heeded. But when we feel emotionally pummeled, we come face to face with something in ourselves that we are in need of opening to, not running from.

BEING JUDGMENTAL INHIBITS OUR ABILITY TO HELP

At one time I hosted a radio show in Los Angeles, and on one program I interviewed a physician whose poignant story I have never forgotten. This chief of pediatrics at a large hospital in Los Angeles county told of a little girl who had changed the way he practiced medicine. The child had been born with a congenitally deformed heart. By the time she was seven, the physician, who was a pediatric cardiologist, had operated on her half a dozen times. The little girl had reached a point where nothing more could be done medically, and she was rapidly growing weaker.

The physician described the judgments and self-criticism that plagued him when the child was in his presence—thoughts that made him want to avoid her: "I can't help her." "I'm useless." "I'm incompetent." "If only I were a better surgeon." "What good are all my years of training?" One day as he was giving the child a routine physical, the nurse suddenly left the examining room.

The little girl seized the moment to ask, "I'm dying, aren't I?"

The physician, too stunned to move, blurted out, "Yes, you are."

At that point something that amazed him happened. The child looked up, smiled, and began to talk to him about death and dying. She told him that she wasn't afraid of dying but was concerned about how her parents were going to feel. She was curious and had many questions that she wanted to ask. They talked for nearly an hour during which time the physician frequently admitted that he didn't know the answers to her questions. By the time the discussion ended, however, the physician knew that he had something of great value to offer his dying patients—interest, attention, and love.

So often our self-judgments block our capacity to be of help to ourselves as well as to others. Patients who repeatedly tell themselves, "I'm no good." "I'm too old." "I'm no longer good looking." "I'm a burden." "I'm not important." waste valuable time and energy. The feelings of fear and vulnerability that underlie compulsive judgments hold the key to overcoming and replacing them with constructive behaviors that support healing and well-being.

SHAME, GUILT, AND PUNISHMENT

From criticism and judgment we slide easily and naturally into shame, guilt, and punishment. "I caused my cancer, my multiple sclerosis, AIDS." "If I had only ____, he/she would not be sick." "If I were more knowledgeable, skilled, talented, they would have recovered."

We feel shame when we do something over which we have no control and that act is judged "bad" or "wrong," such as wetting our pants when we were little. Guilt is a result of "wrongdoings" carried out with intent and conscious control, such as hitting our kid sister when our parents weren't looking, or allowing someone else to take the blame for our mistake.

Shame and guilt that ties into unresolved feelings is characterized by obsessive and compulsive behavior. It is not difficult to openly admit regret or an error in judgment provided no emotional baggage is attached. If we cannot bring ourselves to say we're sorry, it is time to pay attention to unresolved emotions.

HOW EFFECTIVE IS PUNISHMENT?

Belief in punishment for wrongdoing derives from ancient dogma: "An eye for an eye." Punishment takes various forms, the most immediate association usually being physical abuse. We can punish ourselves by overeating, drinking excessively, taking drugs, or mercilessly driving ourselves with work, sports, or sex. There are also numerous ways of inflicting psychological punishment, which can leave even deeper scars. Anger or withdrawal can have profoundly devastating effects. One of the most insidious punishments is that which induces shame or guilt as punishment. As a child, a client of mine had been told that his behavior was so upsetting it had been the cause of his father's heart attack. The guilt he lived with from that time on was so enormous it literally almost destroyed him.

When my first child was five, he started taking loose change and other things he fancied. I gave him the usual lecture about stealing but with no effect. My anxiety increased. The next time he took something that did not belong to him, I spanked him. He responded by stealing behind my back. Not only did punishment not "civilize" him, but I felt like an ineffective bully.

The judgment/punishment cycle limits rather than extends learning. Punishment evokes anger, and we use our anger to push away the pain of guilt or shame. But some pain is often a logical consequence of inappropriate behavior. If we permit ourselves to perceive it, to fully experience it, our discomfort produces self-correction. However, this principle is operative only to the extent that we have remained open and connected to our feelings. The more we shut out feeling, the more out of sync we are with moral realities.

When I stopped making an issue of my son's forays into others' belongings, stealing lost its thrill for him. When he was met with understanding instead of anger and punishment, he began to realize that he was hurting others and to feel bad about his behavior. My punishing him had obscured his capacity to learn his own lessons. I came to the realization that my need to punish him was born of my fear of being a "bad" mother, of producing a son who "steals." We both came to trust each other again.

All forms of punishment elicit anger, decisiveness, and resentment in others and in ourselves. The more we judge, criticize, and punish ourselves, the more our emotional selves go underground and are lost to our consciousness. Punishment is supposed to keep us safe from injury and harm. Yet, ultimately, the only thing judgment and punishment produce is alienation from ourselves.

JUDGMENT AND CRITICISM INVENTORY

I recommend that you bring humor and playfulness into this quiz in order to diminish the likelihood of your becoming critical of your criticism!

MY (BLANK) IS TOO (BLANK)!

Complete the following sentences using one or two words. Do not think about your answers; just let them occur spontaneously.

1. I'm much too _____.
2. I should _____.
3. If I cared about _____, I would _____.
4. I always notice how badly I _____, _____, and _____.
5. I'm not _____ enough.
6. My _____ is too _____.
7. Whenever I _____, I punish myself by _____.
8. I shouldn't _____ so often.
9. If _____ cared for me, he/she would _____.
10. I'm always disappointed with _____.
11. My _____ is not _____.
12. Compared to _____, I'm _____.
13. When I see a child being punished, I feel _____.
14. If I were more _____ and _____, I would _____.

15. When my mother punished me, she would _____.
16. I am being punished for _____.
17. The worst punishment I can think of is _____.
18. I will never learn how to _____.
19. If I were the perfect _____, then I would _____.
20. I feel punished when someone _____ me.
21. Whenever I was punished as a child, I felt _____.
22. My life would be fine if I could just _____.
23. When I cannot do something well, I _____.
24. When my father punished me, he would _____.
25. The thing I criticize others most for is _____.

IN MY OPINION!

Respond to the following. Again, do this rapidly, without thinking about your answers.

1. Men are _____.
2. Women are _____.
3. Old people are _____.
4. Powerful people are _____.
5. Blacks are _____.
6. Whites are _____.
7. Jews are _____.
8. Bisexuals are _____.
9. Homosexuals are _____.
10. Death is _____.

How did you come to these opinions: Experience? Family? Peer Pressure?

PUNISHMENT ASSESSMENT

Respond to each of the following questions.

1. The ways I punish myself are by ＿＿ and by ＿＿ and by ＿＿.
2. The ways I punish others are by ＿＿ and by ＿＿ and by ＿＿.
3. The things I criticize most in others are ＿＿ and ＿＿ and ＿＿.

Look over the lists above. Do you see any correlation between them? Any close similarities or differences? Anything you would care to change? Examine your feelings as you look over the lists.

CRITICISM, JUDGMENT, AND PUNISHMENT INVENTORY

These exercises often expose numbed anger, resentment, or sadness. Allow awareness of such feelings to surface and know that experiencing them will permit access to energy that was formerly used to block awareness.

1. Make a list of all the put-downs you received throughout your childhood. For example, "You're such a slob." "You can't ＿＿ worth a damn." "Aren't you ever going to grow up?" List all the messages you heard from parents, teachers, and other adults that made you feel insecure or inadequate. As you list them, allow the feelings you experienced then to be felt now. Next, list the put-downs you hear from yourself, the critical voice that continues to find fault with your thoughts and ac-

tions. Are there any similarities between the two lists? Consider how long you have been believing these opinions of yourself. Allow your reactions to be felt physically and emotionally.

2. Have a written or imaginary dialogue with the part of you that is the "Critic." Play both the part of you that is the Critic and the part that sincerely wants to understand the need to be critical. Begin by saying something like: "Hello, Critic. Would you please come forward so I can talk with you?" The Critic may answer. "Why would I want to talk with you, you're such a jerk?" No matter what comes up, simply say it without passing judgment. Allow any feelings to surface with the words. You may find yourself assuming different postures with each character. Just allow whatever arises to be aired. Allow the conversation to continue until it finishes itself. Then give yourself a few minutes to reflect on what has been said.

3. Have the Critic write a letter to you. In the letter, let it describe itself physically. Let it tell you why it is present, how it functions, why it puts you down, if it plans to continue. Have the Critic also tell you what you can do to help, what it needs from you, how the two of you can get together to work as a team instead of being adversaries. When you have finished, write a return letter, responding to whatever the Critic has written. This is a most illuminating exercise and an excellent way to help you integrate your critic so that it may support, not undermine you.

4. Repeat Exercise three, using the "internal judge" instead.

5. Think about a time in your life, probably your childhood, when you were punished. Close your eyes and try to

recreate the scene as vividly as possible—the sights, sounds, emotions, the physical sensations you experienced. As you continue to stay with the visualization, allow any feelings you may have to be acknowledged, whether these feelings are the ones you felt then or the ones you are experiencing now. When you are finished, reflect on the feelings that surfaced and forgive yourself now for whatever it was that you had done then.

6. Think about a time when you were punishing. Close your eyes and recreate the moment as completely as you can, especially the deep feelings you were experiencing. Let the scene come to life in your imagination as you allow the emotions to surface in your body. Allow these feelings you had toward that person to be felt right now. Stay with the feelings and acknowledge any anger, guilt, sadness, whatever. When the experience no longer carries an emotional charge when you reflect on it, forgive the punisher.

7. Purchase a golf clicker (sold at most pro shops and sporting goods stores). They are inexpensive. Carry it around with you for a day or two; and whenever you hear yourself criticize or judge, push the button in acknowledgment. You may wish to use the clicker whenever you feel like punishing. Use it for only one or the other at a time. This is an exercise to see just how many times you feel the necessity to criticize or punish. The very act of pushing the button, of acknowledging that you have been critical, takes the edge off your action and makes it easier to observe yourself with compassion. Eventually you will not have to use a clicker to acknowledge your feelings. Just noticing will be the "click."

CHAPTER 4

Observation and Acceptance

"But before I look out . . .
let me first gaze within myself."
—Rainer Maria Rilke

The previous chapter provided you with the opportunity to become more familiar with some of your favorite blind spots. I hope that it also encouraged you to begin smiling at a few of your foibles. This chapter represents a continuation and deepening of this point of view. In order to begin overcoming limiting habits and patterns, we must do two things. We must first find the courage to become aware of our feelings, thoughts, and behaviors—and then compassionately accept our findings.

A woman came up to me after a seminar I had led and quietly said, "I would like to tell you something. I have been in physical pain for many years with a condition that doesn't seem to respond to treatment. I have never been advised to do anything other than try to forget it or take so many painkillers that I can barely function. Or they tell me to focus on the 'good' things in life. It always sounded like good advice—you know, think positively."

"Did thinking positively take the pain away?" I asked.

"No," she laughed, "but it did make it less painful for others to be around me! I just wanted you to know that I tried something different today."

She looked at me expectantly, as though she was ready to burst with a wondrous secret.

"Do you want to tell me about it?"

"Oh, yes!" she said excitedly. "In the exercises today I permitted myself to focus on my pain, as you suggested. I was very afraid at first, but I just made myself get into the place that hurt. It was very scary at first, though. I didn't know what to expect." She stood silently, thoughtfully.

"What happened then?" I asked softly.

"My God, you'll never imagine. For the first time in years I sat comfortably. I could put my attention on something other than trying to forget about how bad I felt." Tears filled her eyes.

"I feel radiant now, absolutely radiant," she continued, tears streaming down her face. "I feel strong, healthy—as if I could take on anything—and I feel like hugging everyone," at which point this rather large woman scooped me up into her arms for a long and intense bear hug. In her embrace I could feel the relief and the love as it poured out of her.

I do not relate this story to suggest that by focusing on that which we dread we can change our lives forever. I imagine that a day, week, or month later this same woman awoke one morning to the pain so familiar to her and once again felt overwhelmed by it. I tell the story, instead, to make the point that the experience of observing, acknowledging, and accepting what we fear not only frees us but empowers us as well. The woman at the seminar is free not because she will never have to experience distress again, but because she can respond to her discomfort actively, by choice, in a way that will enhance her dignity and self-respect.

The previous chapter provided you with the opportunity to become more familiar with some of your favorite blind spots. I hope that it also encouraged you to begin smiling at a few of your foibles. This chapter represents a continuation and deepening of this point of view. In order to begin overcoming limiting habits and patterns, we must do two things. We must first find the courage to become aware of our feelings, thoughts, and behaviors—and then compassionately accept our findings.

CAREFUL OBSERVATION LEADS TO CHANGE

I was dramatically introduced to the principle of uncritical observation years ago in a group lesson from Tim Gallwey, author of *The Inner Game of Tennis*. Tim taught us to focus on exactly what we were doing without correcting us or making us feel wrong in any way. He had the group watch him, without telling us what he was doing. For a while he just kept hitting ball after ball. Then he asked each of us to mimic what he had been doing. As we did, we began to notice that we were moving very differently from the way he moved. Person after person, men and women, young and old, began modifying their stance, follow-through, etc. Tim started hitting balls randomly to the group, and we were able to hit almost every one of them back to him—even placing a few where we wanted them to go!

This approach gave me the opportunity to observe uncritically, to notice old reflexive approaches, and to make corrections based on "how it feels to do it right compared to how it felt to do it wrong." Observation enables us to look at the variety of choices that are available to us in any context.

The state of illness and burnout obscures the fact that choices are at hand. It may seem that no option exists. We may feel trapped and victimized by our health, our responsibilities, our needs. Yet, as observant and compassionate witnesses to ourselves, we see that living or dying are processes that involve us in making many choices— and with observation and acceptance comes the power of intention. We can change. We can test out our fears. We can stay open and explore, or close down and run. We are the ones in charge of our lives! We are not at the mercy of our patterns or victims of ancient programming. Our behavior may not radically change, but by observing and accepting all there is to know about ourselves, we can watch and take a quantum leap forward in our own evolution.

Change contains elements that can be experienced as deathlike. This can be very frightening. The choice to feel physically and emotionally is a choice toward abandoning safety for the promise of renewed vitality. It is also a commitment to letting go of our suppositions about who and what we are as we learn to observe and accept who and what we find.

We have spent a lifetime selectively amassing "truths" about who we are from family, friends, teachers, employers, and "experts." We have grown up on conditional relationships—"If you—clean your room; get straight A's; graduate from college; make more money; go to bed with me; say you're sorry; love me—I'll love you in return." We have been protecting ourselves since infancy from the real or imagined threat of loss of love and loss of self. Though our reasons for self-protection may seem numerous and valid, they only provide an illusion of safety that keeps us reacting in ways that are inappropriate and unproductive. Because we believe our choices are so limited and our need for safety is so great, we have been unwilling to change. Even now change may appear to be impossible, but it is not. Transformation begins with a willingness to observe ourselves uncritically.

RESEARCHING YOURSELF

But change what and when and how? Before you can formulate intentions, you must first assess the situation. Since you can be reasonably assured that the problem has something to do with you, your decision to do things differently should begin with a research project on yourself— your raw materials, your attitudes, your values, and your behaviors. Only by understanding the choices you have made and continue to make can you begin to add new, more satisfying options.

Most intentions to change are predicated upon the shaky foundation of inaccurate self-knowledge. You now need to explode the self-limiting childhood myths, your less-than-objective opinions of others, the restricting stereotypic models that society and the media have provided, and your own nearsighted view about who and what you are. This research project, with you as the subject, will involve learning simply to observe yourself, much like an inquiring reporter—compassionately, without the hindrance of criticism. You have been watching yourself all your life, of course, but as a judge—and a hanging judge, no doubt. You also have been watching from a perspective that most likely includes many suppositions and belief systems that may not be fully accurate. But please note: You will not continue to observe yourself if you heap judgment, blame, and guilt on top of the incoming information. When our feelings and actions are continually labeled as bad or wrong, it becomes too painful and frustrating to continue.

Do not be surprised if you find this process difficult at first. Ignoring judgment and criticism is difficult enough, but replacing them with curiosity, understanding, and humor whenever possible, may be tantamount to gleefully submitting to a root canal. Just keep at it. Soon you will begin to notice that you are taking yourself far less seriously. And the longer you stay with the process, the easier it will get.

REMAINING HONEST WITH YOURSELF

The rule, remember, is simply to watch and acknowledge. Observe and accept all that you perceive, all that you feel. A simple example is an exchange that occurs frequently between most couples. He/She (tentatively): "You seem distant. Anything wrong?" She/He (looking away, tense, tight-lipped): "No, nothing."

There are many variations on this same theme. Both persons know that one is lying but would rather not risk talking about "it," and that the other is too afraid to risk pursuing the subject in case they are involved. So they both ignore "it."

You can now watch your own reaction patterns of unwillingness to share your feelings and consciously acknowledge them, if not yet directly to your partner, then to yourself. How do you feel emotionally? Scared, angry, sad? How do you feel physically? Remember your body is the great clearinghouse of physical, emotional, and intuitive information. Have you tensed your body anywhere, held your breath? Does your throat ache, is your stomach tight? Acknowledge your feelings, your reactions, but do not judge yourself wrong in the process. Just accept whatever you notice. If you feel confident enough, and if your partner is supportive, you may wish to express your feelings to him or her.

When you are in a situation not directly involving another person, such as getting a parking ticket, getting lost in an unfamiliar part of town, or running out of gas, again simply notice and acknowledge to yourself how you feel—angry, tense, frightened, depressed. Then get on with finding a gas station.

And do not forget to notice your positive emotions and physical feelings. What thoughts and behaviors are connected to these? Allow yourself your happiness, your joy, your elation, and let that be okay. If you have difficulty giving them a place in your life, notice that, too.

As you objectively learn to watch and assess your true feelings, wants, needs, and actions, you will recognize values and beliefs, habits and emotions, that you did not realize you had. Others you may have expected to have will seem significant by their absence. It is precisely through this blend of observation and feeling, data and emotion, that a greater level of wisdom and sensitivity emerges, one based more on fact than fantasy, more on reality than myth. You are learning how you feel.

THE ART OF COMPASSIONATE OBSERVATION

The art, or zen, of observation is related to our ability to process our feelings at an experiential level. When feeling takes place in the body, our minds remain clear and our hearts open. "Detachment," far from being a state of uninvolvement is a state of acute involvement. As detached observers, we are able to both accurately and compassionately comprehend everything about ourselves: "Oh, I'm smiling, but I feel like crying." "Oh, I'm seething inside and wolfing my food down." "Oh, I'm pretending that everything is okay, but it's not!" We comprehend it all—the feelings, the motivations, the behaviors—and it's okay.

From this perspective surprising and even amazing truths come to light. We begin to see that all our behaviors are reasonable to some degree including those that don't appear to be. For example, through careful, uncritical observation we can begin to see that there are advantages to illness or burnout. These might include: attention; care; release from an intolerable person, job, or situation; or permission to say no when we want to. Subtleties like these cannot be perceived with either a critical mind or a closed heart, but their recognition plays an important role in renewal and recovery.

Compassion is not sympathy. There may be times when we justifiably feel sorry for ourselves or others. However, when this is the case, we are not in the observer state and we have temporarily lost our objectivity. Compassion does not require us to be sympathetic, because in the absence of criticism and judgment, we remain emotionally open and mentally clear. A balance is struck between caring and discerning.

The following story is an account of a courageous young woman who has been able to strike that balance by substituting determination for self-pity or bitterness.

Olivia ended her marriage with the intention of avoiding men permanently and during the years her son Enrichi was young, she maintained her resolve. However, when Enrichi became less of a full-time responsibility, Olivia's loneliness surfaced and it was then that she met Tomas.

Tomas treated Olivia differently than other men had. He was gentle and respectful. He was also eight years her junior, which initially concerned Olivia, but delighted Enrichi. For the teenager, Tomas was a longed-for older brother.

Enrichi's affection for Tomas assuaged Olivia's misgivings about the difference in their ages, but there was also another matter. Tomas had been involved with the drug scene on the street before they met. However, he no longer hung around with his former pals, and now worked steadily and swore that he was clean.

In the beginning Olivia and Tomas were inseparable. He thought of nothing but her, and she experienced a renewed sense of excitement about life. Tomas asked to move in with Olivia and Enrichi, and though she protested at first, eventually she relented. All went well until a disease of unknown origin began to impact their lives.

The medical facility where Olivia worked was one of the first to do research on AIDS. Thus, while the rest of the country was focusing on AIDS as "the gay disease", Olivia knew better. She was aware that intravenous needle-sharing invited as great a risk to acquiring the dread disease as sexual transmission. This information gave her cause to worry as she knew that Tomas had shared needles in the past.

Olivia innocently suggested to Tomas that he be tested, and was stunned by the vehemence of his response. Tomas, angrily interpreted her suggestion as an insinuation that he was "gay or bisexual," and refused to discuss the subject. Olivia reminded Tomas that he had shared needles when he was on the streets and urged him to be tested. His response was to threaten to leave her if she continued to press the subject. "Neither of us is sick,," he told her. "Why are you trying to ruin things?"

Olivia was devoted to Tomas and did her best to put the subject of AIDS out of her mind, but her work-setting brought the subject to mind on a daily basis. Olivia knew that one can carry the AIDS virus for years and transmit it to others without exhibiting symptoms, and this deeply worried her. Finally, she couldn't stand the suspense any longer and had herself tested.

Olivia *was* HIV positive, and that meant that Tomas was also positive, because she had not received blood or been with anyone but Tomas for years. This knowledge and the very different ways that each chose to respond to it ended their relationship.

Though she felt fine, Olivia couldn't stick her head in the ground and pretend that everything was as it had been. She had to acknowledge the possibility of becoming gravely ill in the future and perhaps dying. She also had to do everything in her power to avoid this possibility.

Olivia sought out therapy for the emotional support that she needed. This helped her to realize that, if nothing else, Tomas had awakened in her the realization that she was a vital woman with a great deal to share and live for. With or without Tomas, Olivia's commitment was to life! Of course Olivia knew that now she, like Tomas, had the potential of infecting others with the HIV virus. She had to be very careful, but while the prospect of developing AIDS frightened her, the knowledge that she could avoid infecting someone else was a comfort.

Informed by her counseling experiences, Olivia reasoned that the more discerning she became about her behavior, the better her chances for remaining well. To this end she became a compassionate observer of everything that she did, including her inner processes, her habits, and outer activities. At the close of each day, as well as several times during the day, she paused to take account of all that she observed.

In the context of honestly affirming her feelings, Olivia acknowledged the hurt, anger, and sense of outrage she felt toward Tomas, but she also took responsibility for bringing him into her life. She acknowledged that the instinct that had prompted her to seek love and companionship deserved her respect and attention.

With the aid of a carefully constructed health program, Olivia remains well and in control of her life. While her routine changes from time to time, her guide to well-being continues to be drawn from her power of self-observation. With both focus and compassion, Olivia notes, accepts, and acts on messages her body communicates to her through her feelings.

OBSERVATION IS NOT OBSESSION

I would like to stress the point that watching does not mean examining every nuance of thought, behavior, or feeling. This process is not to become all-consuming self-involvement. If, however, you confront areas in your life that cause a strong physical or emotional reaction—any belief or behavior that creates discomfort for you—this is the place to look. If you are in a conversation with a friend and you suddenly feel like crying; or if you receive a compliment and want to crawl under a table; or if you realize you are in a rage because you cannot find your sunglasses—take note and acknowledge it, and go on about your business. You may not like or even approve of what you notice. Just keep reminding yourself that you are not the judge, you are the reporter. Your job is to learn about yourself, period.

Observation and collection of information about yourself generates one very dramatic change: The choices available to you multiply significantly. Whereas before you may have felt limited, confused, and out of control, you now are able to move in new directions. Watching yourself from a nonjudgmental perspective can help you begin correcting behaviors that have limited you for a lifetime. You cut out the blaming. You stop wasting your life feeling victimized, helpless, and sorry for yourself. And as you grow in openness and understanding, you grow in confidence.

OBSERVE AND ACCEPT INVENTORY

The following questions are intended to get you to grow more self-observing in difficult or intense moments. Answer them as spontaneously as possible. Remember, all answers are valid because they provide useful information. This is especially true of those that do not particularly please you because they point out where work with yourself lies.

INTERIOR ASSESSMENT

1. When my mate wants to do something without me, I _____.
2. If someone I like doesn't like me, I _____.
3. When a loved one forgets my birthday, I assume they _____.
4. When I have done something I'm ashamed of, I _____.
5. When I get what I want, I _____.
6. I don't really feel my best unless I _____.
7. When I lose control of myself, I _____.
8. I can't turn off my thoughts when _____.
9. When I'm jealous, I _____.
10. When I'm frightened, I _____.
11. When I'm depressed, I _____.
12. When I'm at a gathering of people I don't know, I usually _____.
13. When I'm in a conversation about which I know very little, I _____.
14. When I make a mistake, I _____.
15. I show love most often by _____.

SECONDARY GAINS

The following is a list of "good reasons" for becoming ill or burned out. Do you identify with any of the benefits on this list?

1. People are nicer to me.
2. I don't have to work.
3. I don't have to answer to him or her.
4. I have an excuse for saying no.
5. I can punish him/her/them.
6. I don't have to think about the future.
7. I don't have to grow old.
8. I don't have to be responsible.
9. People care more for me.
10. I don't have to force life.

- Did you struggle over any of these questions? If you did, consider the possibility that you are undecided about your answer.
- Is there a down side to these "advantages"?
- List the possible disadvantages connected to a true answer to any of the above.

Answer the following questions very rapidly and spontaneously. What you're after is an observation of how accepting of yourself and others you really are.

TELLING THE (OOPS) TRUTH!

N = Never R = Rarely S = Sometimes F = Frequently
A = Always
1. When I feel left out or ignored it ____ troubles me.

2. It ___ upsets me when a stranger behaves in a less than friendly manner toward me.
3. I ___ beat myself up for making a mistake.
4. When I have done something I'm ashamed of, I ___ admit it publicly or privately.
5. I ___ expect to be at my best.
6. I can ___ laugh at my vulnerabilities and inconsistencies.
7. I ___ recognize my blind spots and imperfections without feeling guilty.
8. If someone gets mad at me it ___ spoils my day.
9. I ___ feel that I should know more.
10. I ___ have to have the "last word."

ASSESSING THE TRUTH

Answer the following questions.

1. Are you comfortable with the way others see you? Explain.
2. Are you comfortable with the way you see yourself? Explain.
3. Do you feel that you would have to make substantial changes in order to qualify as lovable? Explain.
4. What do you find most difficult to accept about yourself at this time?
5. Were you more or less accepting as a child?

WHO ARE YOU?

1. For sixty seconds, list any words that come to you that you believe describe you. Let the words flow spontaneously, without evaluating them.

2. Read over the words. Are there any recurring themes? Do any words evoke a strong reaction?
3. List the five qualities you most enjoy about yourself.
4. List the five qualities you least enjoy about yourself.
5. Put a check next to the ones for which you feel others least enjoy you.
6. Put a star next to the ones you feel are the most difficult for you to accept about yourself at this time.

WATCHING THE PICTURE SHOW INSIDE YOUR HEAD

The following exercise will help you to become aware of your thought patterns.

1. Decide to begin paying careful, objective attention to your daytime mind pictures.
2. Ask yourself the following questions: What are the scenarios that I create—the discussions, situations, and people I love and hate, win and lose within my mind's eye?
3. View these pictures and plots as if you were watching a series of short-subject films during the day.
4. Do this for a week.
5. What do your fantasies tell you about the things you want and need?
6. Note-taking will quicken your awareness as will sharing these stories out loud with a friend. Again, remember to remind yourself to withhold judgment of that which you experience.
7. Keep in mind that "seeing" does not necessarily require a visual experience. You may sense or hear rather than see with your mind's eye. If you have

been watching yourself imagining for a week and taking notes, you can begin to start perceiving patterns—themes that recur. Ask yourself what scripts are replayed and what feelings are generated by these imaginings, particularly the ones you rerun again and again. Note the correlation between the thought process and the feeling.

MY FACE—THE MIRROR OF MY INNER WORLD

The following exercise will help you to begin perceiving the mirror-like relationship between your body and your thoughts and feelings.

1. Take a good look at your face in the mirror right now. Exactly what do you see? Take a long, careful, and detached look. With a draftsman's eye, study the brow, the area around the eyes, the expression in the eyes themselves. How does the left side differ from the right? What about the mouth—the puckers and lines surrounding it? Does your mouth turn up or down? How does one side differ from the other?
2. Ask yourself the following questions, writing down the answers:
   • What does this face that is your face suggest or express?
   • What is its mood?
   • If you met this face in a crowd, how would you react to it?
   • Is this a face—an expression—that you would move toward, that you would feel safe with, or is it a face suggestive of fear, pain, or distrust?
   • Is it rested or tired? Tense or relaxed?

3. Ask yourself and write down the answers to the following questions: Are there places within my body that are directly connected with parts of my face?
   - Do my eyes or mouth connect to what I experience in my stomach or chest at this minute?
   - What connection can I make between what I see and what I experience myself thinking and/or feeling?
4. Strip and once more observe with detachment this body that is yours. Again slowly, exactingly and with an attitude of curiosity, not judgment—as if you were an artist with a drawing pen in hand—observe what you see: the bone structure; the musculature; the placement of the head on the neck; the positioning of the shoulders, hips, knees, ankles, and feet.
5. Ask yourself:
   - What differences exist between the right and left sides of the body?
   - What story does this body tell, what experiences and attitudes does this form express?
   - How does what I see on the surface reflect attitudes and emotions from within?
   - Is it possible to conceive of the inner structures of this form—tissue, muscle, organs, etc.—as also being expressive of thoughts and emotions?

If you get tired of looking at yourself in the mirror, you might begin to look carefully at others in the same way, verifying whenever possible your assumptions about what feelings, thoughts, or attitudes underlie the physical form.

IS THE UNIVERSE FRIENDLY?

1. Make yourself comfortable sitting or lying down and take a few breaths.
2. Ask yourself the following questions with as much detachment as possible:
   - Is the universe personally friendly, unfriendly, or indifferent to me? If your choice was "indifferent" or "unfriendly" continue on.
   - What is the difference between an indifferent and an unfriendly universe?
   - Why do I believe the universe to be unfriendly or indifferent?
   - At what age did I first view the universe as unfriendly or indifferent?
   - How do I protect myself from the hostility or coldness of this unfriendly or indifferent universe?
3. Compassionately accept whatever conclusions you have drawn from this exercise. They represent an honest evaluation of your feelings and beliefs at this moment.

CHAPTER 5

Wanting Vs. Needing

> *"As long as I'm trying to decide,*
> *I can't feel what I want to do."*
> —Hugh Prather

The more we learn about honesty and self-acceptance, the more aware we become of the gaps between what we long for and what we actually pursue. The following stories point to the fact that most of us fail to differentiate between what we believe we want and what we actually need in order to feel good.

Irene, a strikingly beautiful woman executive in her mid thirties, came into my office for marriage counseling with her husband, Carl, who accompanied her reluctantly. Bright and articulate, Irene listed with genuine feeling all that she wanted but was not getting from her marriage. According to Irene, Carl withheld both money and affection, did not share his thoughts and emotions, and never seemed interested in hers. Finally, she spoke of desperately wanting children, whereas Carl has no such desire, fearing the responsibilities involved.

Carl adored Irene. She was the most stimulating and

exciting woman he had ever known, and he appreciated her intelligence and beauty. Despite the ongoing verbal abuse she heaped upon him, he was willing to explore his motives and, if possible, alter his behavior in order to make her happy. This process was difficult for Carl, and he struggled every step of the way. Nevertheless, he made significant strides in overcoming his fears and altering a lifelong pattern of distrust.

Carl began to support Irene in the ways she had requested. Irene became pregnant as she had wished. However, her experience of their relationship did not change. She now had all that she had said she wanted from Carl, yet she continued to find fault with him, continued to feel dissatisfied and unfulfilled.

Carl, though at first skeptical of his need for self-exploration, gained in confidence to the point that he felt unwilling to submit to criticism from Irene. In the end, it was Carl's insistence that Irene change *her* behavior toward *him* that finally produced a relationship that satisfied Irene.

Growing up, Stan had very little contact with his father and perhaps that was why being "one of the boys" was so important to him. While maintaining excellent grades in high school, he also devoted himself to drinking, smoking, and racing cars. A similar pattern was repeated later during his college years when taking drugs at parties was added to the list of misbehaviors that equated "acting out" with "manly independence." Following graduation Stan took a managerial job in a local seaport where he made friends with some of the rowdier men on the dock. His evenings were spent bar-hopping and womanizing, and sometimes these outings included sharing needles and trips to local houses of prostitution.

Stan's abundance of energy kept him going night and day for several years. He didn't get much rest, but all went well until the outbreak of AIDS. Accounts of "high risk behavior" gave him reason to be concerned about his own past. Though he felt healthy Stan voluntarily tested for the AIDS virus and braced himself for the results, which were positive.

At twenty-eight Stan had some serious thinking to do. At the time very little was known about AIDS, and in the part of the country where he lived, there were few resources available. California appeared to be the state where the most AIDS activity was taking place, but Stan questioned whether he dared make such a move at such a time. He decided to take the risk and relocate in an area where he could be more actively involved in maintaining his health. Fortified only with a list of health-care professionals who he hoped would see him, Stan abandoned the comfort and safety of his familiar surroundings. Without knowing a soul in L.A., but feeling good about having the courage it took to make the move, he found a place to stay and employment.

Stan researched and absorbed all the information he could about autoimmune disease. He consulted doctors, took classes and seminars, and experimented with a variety of self-help groups. In addition, he read everything on the subject that he could find. Moreover, he began integrating this learning into day-to-day activities, and started to pay serious attention to his feelings and the quality of his life.

Being a "bad boy" made Stan feel high temporarily, but it did not fill the void that he often felt when he was alone. Moreover, the price he paid for "fun" had been far too high. In subsequent months, he came to understand and accept the feelings of loneliness and isolation that had motivated his reckless behavior.

Stan was a social animal. Playful and outgoing, he loved camaraderie and was genuinely interested in people. However, there were many ways to satisfy his social needs without threatening his own life. Ironically, while Stan's desire to be one of "the boys" had gotten him into serious trouble, his courageous response to discovering that he was HIV-positive produced the self respect he had sought but had never been able to secure.

During the years that Stan has known that he is HIV-positive, he has had many opportunities to question the differences between his wants and needs. With a deeply felt desire for life and health guiding him, Stan has learned to discern between what makes life more pleasurable, and what is merely an attempt to avoid pain. Knowing this difference helps him to remain well.

In her youth, Alice had more suitors than she ever had time for. Throughout her twenties and early thirties, she bounced from one eligible man to the next. Not that Alice was a superficial person. Intense, curious, and creative, she pursued a wide range of interests, traveled extensively, and experienced life as endlessly exciting until she reached her mid thirties. From here on, the crop of suitors rapidly dried up—at exactly the time when she began to long for a family.

Alice joined the ranks of people desperately longing to love and grew lonelier and lonelier in the process. Eventually, in her late forties, after the breakup of a relationship that she considered to be her last hope for domestic fulfillment, Alice gave up trying. Instead of devoting herself to finding a suitable mate, she turned her attention toward the spiritual interests that had drawn her for years but which she had never fully explored. Alice became deeply involved in the spiritual life of an orthodox community. Within this context, she found peace and the sense of fulfillment that had eluded her for years.

At this point, she met Reighley, who like herself had never been married. Reighley too was a "seeker," looking for purpose and meaning in life. In the process of learning to set aside individual desires, the two fell in love, although nearly a year passed before they made this discovery. Once they did, however, it took them no time to decide to marry. In the context of looking beyond herself and feeling content with her aloneness, Alice finally found the mate she had wanted—and a great deal more.

At thirty-nine, Jim was a successful banking executive with a wife and two nearly grown children. The son of a minister, Jim was a loving father, a devoted husband and a community leader who sang in the church choir on Sundays. Prosperous and accomplished, beloved and admired, Jim should have been a happy and fulfilled man. He certainly had everything he wanted. He had made all the "right choices" based on the values that he had grown up with.

However, Jim was facing a problem that seriously threatened his life. His doctor put it bluntly: "Jim, you're a stroke ready to happen." Jim's blood pressure had reached a dangerously high level and the medications intended to lower it had proved ineffective. In the absence of a medical solution, his doctor suggested psychotherapy, knowing that Jim drank heavily and was very tense. As

Jim put it: "I had no choice but to get in touch with my feelings."

There was a wall of tension and numbness to penetrate. But once he got through the layers of denial, there was no questioning the fact that Jim was a homosexual. Clues had surfaced throughout his life, but he had not dared to face their consequences. As a child and adolescent, he'd had secret crushes on other boys. Before his marriage he'd had a couple of brief homosexual affairs that his wife, in fact, knew about. But they both pretended these "isolated experiences" didn't mean anything.

"I drank in order to dull my thoughts and feelings," he said. "Though occasionally, when I was on a business trip, I would wake up beside another man." Jim didn't want to hurt the children he loved or the fine woman of whom he said, "She would surely have made me into a heterosexual if any woman could have."

Jim had wanted so much to be "normal" and to adhere to the values of his family, his suburban community, and his church that he had ignored his needs and his true self. The choices he made were based on his perceived values, but they didn't support his health or well-being. What he needed really frightened him and appeared to threaten everything he had spent his life trying to achieve. Nevertheless, he found the courage to rethink his values and change his priorities. He found the strength and faith to tell his entire family the truth; to get a divorce; to move to a city where he could seek employment in the banking world as an openly gay man; and to find a male partner to share his life with. By paying attention to his feelings, Jim fulfilled his needs.

Today, at forty-nine, Jim says, "I have a wonderful, wonderful life and I wouldn't trade places with anyone.

I'm loving myself and being myself." Jim's health is excellent.

THE DIFFERENCE BETWEEN WHAT WE THINK AND WHAT WE DO

It's not at all uncommon for individuals to believe in one set of values and practice another. In a complex culture like ours, we grow up getting confusing or mixed messages about what to want. "Have a good time," but, "never lose control." "Money isn't everything," but, "cheat on your income tax if you can get away with it." "Be accommodating," but, "don't be a pushover." Parents tell us one thing, friends another; teachers, heroes, the media—all tell us something else.

The choices we make in terms of what we want, what we do, how we spend our time, who we spend our time with, may not be reflective of what we believe is important. These choices may actually reflect our attempts to preserve emotional protection. We extol the virtues of love, relationship, commitment, dedication—even honesty, and yet consistently behave in ways that are contrary to these "beliefs."

To some it might appear that we are hypocrites in light of the variance between our values and actions, but we are not. The disconnection between what we think and do is directly related to the disconnection between what we think and what we feel. This imbalance is responsible for the confusion. As we learn how to experience our feelings, we come to understand the place of fear and protectedness in our lives. It becomes obvious that these, rather than our values, are often the real driving force behind many of the choices we make. Though it may seem that we're making all the "right moves," in fact, we have been building protections from facing emptiness or low self-esteem.

By disconnecting from the feeling part of ourselves it is easy to reflect beliefs that we may not even approve of, let alone like. Frequently, the values that underlie these beliefs mirror those of our families or people we admire, envy, or look up to. An ironic benefit of testing positive for any major physical illness is that many people have to get off the fast lane and slow down. They have to abandon overworking, frequent partying, rich foods, recreational drugs, alcohol—any activity that doesn't promote health. Guess what? People not only feel better after such adjustments, they often find that they enjoy life more. Former fast-lane addicts often discover that there is a vast difference between what they thought they wanted and what they have come to feel they really need. Often they begin to find great pleasure in the peace and quiet, or delight in newly formed drug- and alcohol-free friendships and relationships. They often even find they like themselves a lot better!

THE DIFFERENCE BETWEEN WHAT WE WANT AND WHAT WE NEED

Tuning to our physical and emotional feelings brings into focus the deeper value of our actions and helps us better distinguish between what we think we desire and what we actually need. When my child was twelve she told me one day that she had cheated at school but had discovered that she felt terrible afterward. She thought that what she had really wanted was an easy A. But because she was in tune with her feelings, she found she had lost something of greater value, her self-respect, something she needed!

Wants and desires are conceptualizations that relate to our beliefs and values. I want to look like, act like, feel like: Christie Brinkley, Arnold Schwarzenegger, Bruce Springsteen, Wonder Woman, Gandhi, U2, my best friend, my Latin teacher; I want to have a Porsche, a Rolex, a bigger boat, more perks at the office, a $100,000-a-year salary, more hair, less fat, a house at the beach, security, popularity. Desires vary enormously from culture to culture—even from one part of town to another. One man or woman's "style" is another's "gaudy monstrosity." Appreciation of taste, beauty, and fashion vary with the eye of the beholder. Even within the same person, desires can and do shift dramatically all the time.

A need, on the other hand, is a "felt experience"; something a person cannot do without. Needs maintain and sustain life. They ignore cultural and social boundaries. All people share similarities in their dependence upon relatively few basic necessities. Some needs, however, are more commonly acknowledged and understood than others. Most people readily accept their physical needs for sufficient food and protection from the elements. Psychological and spiritual needs, though, often go unseen and unmet—the need to love and to be valued; the need to contribute to life; the need to feel at one with a larger continuum. These, too, are basic needs. But we have been taught either to ignore these needs, to hate the dependency that needs impose upon us, or to believe in the futility of ever satisfying them.

Life itself is often the tragic price we pay for choosing to deny ourselves what we must have. Obviously, we will die faster from lack of water than from lack of emotional security or spiritual connectedness. But when we're lacking any basic human need, we eventually lose hope and the will to continue, which initiates a degenerative process.

The precise ways we meet our needs vary from individual to individual, though the needs themselves do not. The need for good health can be met by eating a variety of foods that supply basic nutritional requirements. The need for recognition and appreciation may or may not be met by a hug, a promotion, a present, a kind word, an M & M, or a gold watch, but somehow this need for self-worth must be filled. Because we are social creatures, we need the support and occasional succor of others. Babies do not fully develop intellectually, physically, or psychologically unless they receive loving physical attention. They may even die if deprived of it. Food and shelter alone are not enough to sustain life.

What we need is far more necessary than what we desire in order to maintain a healthy and vital life. However, we can become so closed down that we cannot differentiate between what is life-sustaining and what is not. The following stories exemplify a theme I've heard repeatedly from individuals who were ill or burned out: "I've lived my life to please or impress others."

Donna had a nonstop life. Her days were filled with housekeeping, meal planning, cooking, gardening, exercising, and careful supervision of her two young children. Four nights a week she taught classes at the local junior college. Her weekends were absorbed by her husband, children, and the load of paperwork she took home every Thursday night.

Donna prided herself in the fact that she managed all

of this on her own. She rarely if ever asked for help even when it was offered. Donna's mother would have been more than happy to babysit or provide getaway time for Donna and her husband, but Donna refused her mother's offers. Donna felt that her mother was too permissive with her grandchildren, and thus she preferred to "do it all herself." She even refused her husband Herb's offers to help her out.

Donna couldn't have been more shocked when she discovered that she had breast cancer. She had always been exceptionally healthy and conscientious about exercising regularly and "eating right." Moreover, Donna felt very positive about all aspects of her life—or so she thought. The books that she read when she was first diagnosed led her to believe that something might be missing in her life, but she couldn't imagine what that "something" might be.

However, in the course of setting some quiet time aside for herself, Donna came to understand that what was missing from Donna's life was Donna! Time to think her own thoughts and feel her own feelings was something that Donna believed she had no right to take. As a girl growing up in a single-parent household she had never seen her mother sit down, and Donna had reflexively followed this example, although she was surrounded by people who were more than willing to help her out.

Donna's experience with surgery and chemotherapy forced her to take stock of herself and realize how much she longed for time to be responsible to no one but herself. Donna, who is alive and well today, has learned to graciously accept and ask for help. She has also learned how to insist on taking some time solely for herself on a regular basis.

* * *

Steve was bright, attractive, and talented. He had a glamorous, well-paying job that kept him flying all over the world. He also had a lover and many friends that he entertained frequently and lavishly. In fact, Steve spent most of the money he made on pleasing and impressing others. He bought elaborate presents, gave extravagant dinner parties, and was always the first to pick up the tab or help out a friend or acquaintance with a money problem. He also ate rich foods, drank and smoked heavily, and took recreational drugs. He believed in the value of his life-style and enjoyed its fast-paced glamor; at least he did until he fell ill with ARC.

Following the diagnosis, his life changed radically. He was fired from his job and left almost penniless, since he had no savings. Once the parties were over, many of his "friends" stopped calling. Steve's lover, however, remained steadfast and devoted. In fact, he quit his own high-pressure job in order to spend more time with Steve. Though they had lived together for years, this was the first time they had really ever talked, planned for the future, or just sat in the same room together listening to music or watching TV.

Together, they conceived of a plan to build a small business in order to support themselves. The enterprise, which required only a partial investment of time, did well, enabling them to live modestly, but comfortably. With so much time on their hands, they began doing volunteer work. Steve, for whom a high salary had always been the mark of satisfying his desire for self-worth, was amazed at the degree of good feeling he derived from helping others.

In the absence of a distracting, fast-paced life, and with

time to experience his feelings and know his mind, Steve discovered a side of himself that he never knew existed. He learned to exercise, eat selectively, and fully enjoy the simplest of activities. He experienced both loving and being loved. His health stabilized. In the process, he found not only a new set of values but a new way of life that proved to be far more personally fulfilling as well as health and life-supporting.

Many of us are like Steve. As a result of losing touch with our feelings we have also lost touch with our needs. There is a popular questionnaire that asks people to list the ten activities they most often enjoy doing, and then to consider how recently and often they do them. You might want to make such a list at this point. Ask yourself what activities provide you with the greatest pleasure in your life. Can you make a list of up to ten items? Now, as you look over your list, note how often during the week you have involved yourself in any or all of your "favorite things."

Most people discover they seldom do the things they feel like doing. Many people, in fact, believe they should feel guilty if they enjoy what they are doing. As a friend sadly says, "If I enjoy doing it, then it must be fattening, illegal, or immoral." What we fail to take into consideration is that when we consistently ignore our needs, we are slowly (or perhaps rapidly) undermining our health and well-being.

Focusing on our physical and emotional feelings, including those that are, at times, painful, can prove invaluable in directing us toward our true needs. Knowing what makes us feel fulfilled, and accommodating our desires accordingly, enables us to use our energies appropriately and economically. In this way we avoid the pursuit of goals that are deleterious to us. By staying in touch with felt needs, we can use our resources fully and in ways that will ensure a lifetime of fulfillment.

VALUES AND CHOICES INVENTORY

DESIRES ASSESSMENT

Now it is again your turn to devote yourself to your research project. This time you are trying to clarify the relationship between desires and needs in your life. Begin to ask yourself the following questions: "What are my true needs?" "How important to me are the things that I want compared to the things that I need?" "Do the things that I want support or conflict with my needs?" "Am I protecting myself from the frustration or sadness of acknowledging a need that I believe cannot be met?" The more emotional you become as you tackle this project, the more you will get out of it. It may even save your life!

WHAT I CAN'T LIVE WITHOUT

Without thinking about each entry, circle the items on the list that strike you as something you cannot live without. Do not let your judgment or criticism interfere with your honesty.

Cigarettes	A mate
Love	Therapy
A new car	A family
Good health	Vacations

Self-respect	Time for yourself
Food	Tension
Popularity	A sense of purpose
Children	Luxury
A satisfying sex life	Beauty
Financial security	A housekeeper
Fame	Music
Job satisfaction	Laughter
A beautiful house	Outdoors experiences
Comfort	A spiritual life
Drugs	Money
A television set	A tan
Nurturing	Fashionable clothing
A job	Friends
Self-expression	A secretary
Pets	A lover
Water	Self-control
Esteem of others	Intimacy
Hobbies	Self-love
A home	Credit cards
New ideas/learning	Emotional support

This is by no means a complete list. Please feel free to add your own items to the ones above.

WHAT DO I WANT? WHAT DO I NEED?

To get in touch with what you believe are the differences between wants and needs, fill in each blank with either the word "want" or "need." Do not stop to consider your choice. Once you have completed the quiz, review your answers as might a dispassionate observer. Do some of your choices surprise you?

1. I _____ to be first.
2. I _____ to be approved of.
3. I _____ to be the center of attention.
4. I _____ to look good.
5. I _____ to dress fashionably.
6. I _____ to be in control at all times.
7. I _____ to have money to live well.
8. I _____ to take care of my body.
9. I _____ to enjoy myself.
10. I _____ to feel well.
11. I _____ to share my true feelings.
12. I _____ to laugh and play.
13. I _____ to feel good about myself.
14. I _____ to have a nice car.
15. I _____ to be creative.
16. I _____ friends.
17. I _____ nurturing food.
18. I _____ a satisfying job.
19. I _____ a loving relationship.
20. I _____ opportunities for self-expression.
21. I _____ junk food.
22. I _____ to feel safe and protected.
23. I _____ to live.
24. I _____ to die.

VALUES AND CHOICES EXERCISES

Remember to consult your physical and emotional feelings for the most factual information in the exercises that follow.

REFLECTING ON VALUES

1. Spend a few minutes reflecting on the things you believe you need to live long and well, focusing on your feelings as well as on your thoughts. Then list ten things that you feel are indispensable to your continued well-being.
2. Place a check by the needs you listed above that you feel are not being met at this time.
3. List the ten things you most want. Write down anything that you would like to have, no matter how silly or extravagant it may seem.
4. Put a check next to the wants listed above that you feel you deserve. How many items do you feel you deserve? All of them? Some of them? Compare how deserving you feel with how difficult you think your wants are to obtain.
5. Compare the above two lists of needs and wants. Are there any similarities? Any obvious differences? On another sheet of paper, put your lists in descending order of importance. Are there any significant changes from their original order? How do you feel about what you have observed?
6. Spend one entire day paying attention to how many times you hear yourself say, "I want" or "I need," whether aloud or to yourself. Notice what you want and need most frequently and notice what you actually spend most of your time doing.
7. On a piece of paper, list the ten things you most want to do. On the same piece of paper, list the ten things you most often choose to do. Compare the two lists. Are they the same? Different? What do you feel about the differences? What would you like to change?

CREATING A WITNESS TO THE CHOICES I MAKE

1. Begin by getting yourself a notebook in which you can jot down observations. I prefer a chart form, myself, with two columns—one with the heading, "What am I choosing to do now?" and the other with the heading, "How do I feel about the choice I have made?"
2. Ask yourself, "What am I doing?" Note all that you're involved in. Presumably you're reading this particular passage; what else are you doing—watching TV, daydreaming, or listening to the neighbors fight?
3. Ask your body how you feel doing whatever it is that you're doing. Generally, your mind will tell you what you're doing, and your body will tell you how you feel doing it.
4. Assess the information that you have collected. How do your choices relate to your values of what values influence your choices?
5. Do a "quick check assessment" of the choices that you are making every few days for a week or so.

UNDERSTANDING VALUES

1. Make a list of the choices you repeatedly make that confuse or confound you.
2. Do you see any similarity between this list and the choices that your parents or the people who raised you made?
3. Is it possible that there are substantial "benefits" connected to these choices? If your answer is "yes," list these benefits.

PART III

Facing Fear

CHAPTER 6

Learning To Live With Fear

"What you are afraid of overtakes you."
—Estonian proverb

In Jean-Paul Sartre's play, "No Exit," three people are trapped in a metaphor of personal hell: a bizarre, mirrorless room with locked doors. After they have agonized and argued over their torturous plight, a door suddenly opens—a way into freedom and the unknown. They are free to go but choose, instead, to remain in their now self-imposed cell.

We too may choose freedom—but do we? We can reach out for health, for the warmth and nurturing that only other human beings can provide—but will we? We can reflect, take time for ourselves, relax, enjoy life and the opportunities it presents—but can we? As "self-researchers," we have begun uncovering the knee-jerk responses that clearly diminish the quality of our lives. We can stop responding in ways that block our intentions, our needs, our creativity, our joyousness—but will we? Or will we continue to choose a prison without doors?

111

Ironically, the "way out" necessitates our looking inside ourselves in order to understand the source of limitations that keep us stuck in unhealthy, exhausting, and confining contexts.

The journey within begins at the point of acknowledging the good reasons for our having built protections in the first place. Only compassionate understanding will enable us to tear down our self-imposed confines brick by brick!

WHY DO WE AVOID AWARENESS OF OUR BODIES?

Feeling is both a physical and emotional experience. Being aware of our bodies isn't pleasurable when we're in pain, nor is it easy to pay attention to the physical sensations in a body that is ill or missing parts, but this doesn't explain our cultural determination to avoid feeling. Most people are locked into patterns of emotional avoidance long before they experience physical discomfort. The basis of this patterning is fear and the belief that, "I'll die or go crazy if I experience intense emotions." This is the statement one hears repeatedly when the suggestion is made to focus on emotions like rage, grief, or anxiety. This response is of course absurd, but it reveals a depth of pain that must be taken seriously.

Individuals fear emotional intensity for a number of reasons: To begin with, when we reconnect with emotional and physical sensations, after years of avoiding them, we resurrect powerful memories of the "hurt child" in our past. The experience makes us feel vulnerable and reminds us of events that we have tried to forget. Memories of unresolved loneliness, emptiness, frustration, pain, and fear are tapped when we begin to focus on emotions and sensations in our bodies. We may be afraid that this recall might trigger dangerous or inappropriate behavior toward ourselves or others. It may also seem that our emotions will paralyze our capacity to think clearly, and this further exaggerates the fear of behaving inappropriately.

Finally, we may dread having to face the emotional truth about the choices that we're making in our lives today—choices that may appear to be safe and comfortable but, at a feeling level, are clearly unhealthy. The difficult truth about today's emotional experiences also includes acknowledging the social isolation that diseases like cancer or AIDS impose. This is a society that denies mortality and vehemently avoids those who are reminders of illness and death. It is also a society that denigrates emotions—fear in particular. What we must hold onto in the face of these fears is the fact that *feeling is a lifeline to health* and that, as adults, we are now able to appropriately experience any emotion. By taking a closer look at the origins of our fears we gain a compassionate understanding that enables us to overcome the past.

THE ROOTS OF FEAR

Johnny, who is two and a half, rides his tricycle with blissful abandon. His mother sits in the yard, watching him pedal happily up and down the sidewalk in front of their home. Her next-door neighbor appears and asks to borrow a cup of flour. Thinking she will only be a moment, she tells Johnny imperatively to "stay on the sidewalk," and goes inside with her neighbor to get the flour. The phone rings and she answers it.

Meanwhile, Johnny is thrilled to discover that if he pedals up to the crest of the driveway, he can rocket down the other side, stopping just short of the street. He does this gleefully a couple of times and has topped the crest once more as his mother and her friend reappear. She gasps as she sees him and screams, "Johnny, NO!" just as he begins his downward roll. Startled, he jumps, his feet fall off the pedals, and he rolls out into the middle of the street. He hears the screech of brakes as his tricycle overturns. Moments later, obviously not seriously hurt but scraped and stunned, he is jerked up and smacked repeatedly on the behind as his mother hysterically rebukes him for riding in the street and sends him to his room under a barrage of disapproval. He is also still reeling from the terrifying sight and sound of a car stopping inches away from him.

Today at forty, John continues to react as he did in the past. When he feels disapproved of, or when another person becomes angry and raises his or her voice at him, John withdraws. Emotional intensity frightens him—his own most of all! Perhaps he can let himself feel sad, but anger or rage—never! He closes down and leaves the room. John does not really know why he reacts this way. He simply does.

Of course no one negative experience is the basis for our lifelong protective patterns. These reactions are a product of our childhood perceptions and the quality of care and love we felt from the significant people in our lives. They are also the product of the social pressures we felt while growing up. In any event, our reflexive responses to emotions were established long ago, and further reinforced by later experiences that reaffirmed our expectations. Chapter Four "Observation and Acceptance,'' offered a detailed description of how feelings get and stay lost.

Most fear-based responses are inappropriate and unnecessary today, but we follow along reflexively, still reacting to feelings we locked away years ago. We may repeatedly attempt to behave differently, but fail to obtain our objective. As a result, we often feel helpless to effect real change. This is because it requires a great deal more to change our behavior than just the desire to do so. We are all basically willing to accept personal transformation—but only if it is unthreatening and easy. Yet permanent change is never easy. Down in some deeply buried vault of our being lies the dread that if we allow ourselves to fully experience the emotions we so carefully deny, we will be overwhelmed by their power and lose our ''selves'' forever.

FEAR UNDERLIES PROTECTION

Again and again, as we permit ourselves to open to the source of our most dreaded emotions, fear awaits us—fear of pain, of uncontrollable rage, of worthlessness, of abandonment, of death, of nothingness. Fear arising from the past, but influencing the present, is the good reason behind the protective responses and behaviors that are no longer rewarding yet continue to influence, even to dominate, our lives.

As we come to recognize the fear that underlies and triggers our self-limiting patterns, we grow in understanding and compassion. We are not ''bad''; we are frightened. With this understanding, we see ourselves as we are rather than as we pretend to be. With compassion for ourselves and a willingness to experience fear itself, we take a giant step forward in our transformational journey.

FACING FEAR WHILE YOU ARE FEARFUL

Fear keeps us imprisoned, even when the doors are wide open and we have no known routes of escape. To overcome fear, to control it instead of allowing it to control us, we must choose to meet the challenge of fear itself. But there is only one way out; we must take the first step forward even though we are still afraid. In order to move ahead, we must experience the very things of which we are most fearful.

Were John to spend ten years in traditional therapy to uncover finally—in a moment of triumphant illumination—that he reacts the way he does primarily because of numerous incidents like the tricycle trauma, his established patterns of anger/withdrawal would not suddenly disappear. He would have an insight into the ''why'' of his reactive behavior. And once he gathers enough insights, he may form some basic concepts about his avoidance of pain. But chances are he will still remove himself from his emotions by repeatedly numbing, intellectualizing, or dumping his feelings rather than feeling them.

''WOULDN'T IT BE EASIER TO JUST LOVE OURSELVES?''

A number of questions are evoked by the thought of pursuing feelings that frighten us. ''Why isn't love enough? Can't we just open our hearts and leave the past behind?'' Love would be enough if we could activate it all the time, but there is a very compelling reason why we do not. The powerful flight or fight reflex is automatically triggered by any real or imagined danger. This reflex will create a situation where we may fight or we may run, but that is about all we are capable of doing. Any feeling that consciously or unconsciously triggers the fight or flight reflex will automatically close our minds and shut down our capacity to love. We can fool ourselves into believing that we are never threatened, but our bodies will tell us otherwise.

Recently, a story appeared in the papers about an isolated monk who after spending ten years in an "angerless state of bliss," decided to reenter civilization. Leaving his cave, he journeyed to a village where he ran into a ruffian who provoked his anger. Reflexively, the monk struck out, hitting and killing the man. Love is not enough, because fear can shut us down—and this includes fears we are not aware of.

A similar question with a psychological edge is: "Doesn't self-esteem protect us from becoming emotionally overwhelmed?" Again the answer is the same. Everyone has old vulnerabilities that get triggered from time to time, and no amount of good feeling about ourselves protects us from such moments.

Another line of reasoning expresses concern about the effects of focusing on negativity. "Shouldn't unpleasant feelings like rage or fear of death be avoided?" "Don't we harm ourselves by thinking negatively?" While it is true that negative thinking and negative head trips are disabling, the *experience* of feeling the full range of our emotions is an essential part of a lifeline to recovery and renewal. The process of feeling is life-supporting, and since it is not possible to feel selectively, we must learn how to experience all of our feelings.

Finally, because so many individuals with AIDS are or have been a part of successful twelve-step programs, the question arises "Do we need anything more?" Paradoxically, gaining control over an obsessive habit is accomplished by surrendering individual control. However, once the habit is no longer the focus of living, it becomes possible to reestablish a sense of personal control paired with responsibility. When this process is based on the ability to constantly experience all our feelings—below the bridge of the nose—we access the fullest range of choices and empowerment. We go beyond emotional awareness. By physically experiencing emotion, rather than emoting or thinking about feelings, we can get in touch with the sources of all obsessive behaviors and find more appropriate and creative outlets for them.

FEAR IS A BOTTOM-LINE EMOTION

The statement, "Fear is a bottom-line emotion," refers to the fact that when we avoid emotions like rage or grief, it is really because we are afraid to face a deeper issue in our lives.

Were John to open up to his feelings, he would feel the full impact of the terror lying below his seething anger. What he would experience most profoundly would be his fears of abandonment, of disapproval, and loss of love. He would also become painfully aware that he is afraid to love others. As a child, he was frequently yelled at for his natural curiosity and behavior. The singular example of the tricycle was typical of his childhood. He was often surprised and frightened by his mother's anger, and exiled to his room. At that tender age, however, he had no way of explaining, much less understanding, his mother's behavior—her fears for his safety, her embarrassment in front of others, her need to maintain "control" of her child, her guilt-produced rages. Instead, he doubted and distrusted himself, his perceptions, his feelings. Today, he continues to doubt and distrust both himself and others.

Emotions connected to past experiences and belief systems that no longer work for us often play dominant roles in our present lives. An extreme but particularly powerful example of this is evident in the story of Laura, a young woman battling for her survival.

Laura came to me two years ago, desperate and terrified. She was suffering from bulimia, a compulsive-eating emotional disorder. The bulimic devotes considerable time and effort to planning, buying, and preparing the food for his/her binges; eats beyond capacity; and finally retches and vomits; then repeats the cycle until he/she is spent, both physically and emotionally. Through traditional psychological methods, treatment is lengthy, if at all successful. Bulimia is an elaborate and powerful escape— and Laura had been repeating some form of this behavior since the age of eight. She was then nearly thirty.

Laura worked very hard to experience her feelings before, during, and after her binges. She spoke of great wrenching pain, shooting from the bottoms of her feet through her chest and heart, culminating at the top of her head. She was filled with intense self-loathing.

What she discovered beneath her self-hatred was despair that she had failed to meet any of her parents' expectations in any way. She wished she would die and hoped that she would be found in a pool of vomit, that she would disgrace her parents and make them profoundly sorry for having pressured her as they had.

Now, at last, Laura has given her deepest emotional

and physical feelings permission to surface, to enter the very marrow of her fear and despair. She is beginning to recognize her own self-worth and eagerly continues her self-discoveries. For the first time in her life, Laura has begun to have nurturing and fulfilling relationships. She also has come to understand that her belief in her parents' disapproval and disappointment had been conceived by a child of four or five, and did not necessarily reflect "the truth" as she had been interpreting it.

Laura is reversing a lifelong pattern, as you are. Instead of pushing fear away through her protective reactions, she has opened herself to her deepest feelings, including fear. To her surprise, she neither died nor went crazy, but found, instead, the strength and power within herself to continue. Finally, she has taken control of her life.

WHAT DO WE FEAR

The list could probably drone on forever but the following represents some of the most frequently recognized fears.

1. We fear the loss of love.
2. We fear physical degeneration, disease, loss of energy.
3. We fear pain.
4. We fear the loss of our loved ones.
5. We fear the loss of status, job, material possessions, especially if we believe that our identity is attached to these things.
6. We fear being wrong, looking foolish, being ignorant.
7. We fear anger and rage—our own and others'.
8. We fear death, and we fear dying.

In addition to the fears we readily acknowledge there are those that we do not. These include the following:

1. We fear sex.
2. We fear isolation and loneliness.
3. We fear the loss of purpose and meaning in our lives.
4. We fear the loss of control.
5. We fear the unknown, the untried—this can include feeling good.
6. We fear people who are different than we are.
7. We fear life, its unpredictability and responsibilities.

THE OTHER SIDE OF FEAR

A discussion of the origins of fear can leave one feeling rather overwhelmed—rather like going to the dentist to have, not one, but a mouthful of rotten teeth extracted. Maybe in the long run we'll feel better, but between now and then things look pretty bleak! The next chapter, "Ride the Wild Horse," will offer solace in the form of a process that enables you to confront and overcome your fears. Before we begin, however, it's important to have a clear picture of where the process can take us.

Precisely because there is so much hidden fear in our life, there is also an extraordinary opportunity for revival and renewal connected to facing fear. The truth of this statement has been repeated many times in many contexts. Fairy tales provide us with some of the oldest and most poignant examples of this age-old certainty.

"Beauty and the Beast," along with "The Frog Prince," and other stories of this genre, convey the message well. Enormous rewards await those with the courage to compassionately embrace that which may terrify them. Beauty, the heroine, represents all that is good, noble, and loving. She is forced to leave the safety of her home and live, instead, with the Beast, otherwise her father will die. The Beast, in Beauty's eyes, is a creature whose physical hideousness and fearful power she can hardly bear. Drawing upon all her will and strength, she forces herself to stay with the creature. To her complete surprise, she grows to care for him, sensing the softness and vulnerability beneath his terrifying exterior. Later, as he lies dying, Beauty realizes that she loves the Beast. At that moment the monster transforms, revealing himself to be a handsome prince as the power of Beauty's loving acceptance breaks the spell that has been placed on him. And, as all fairy tales end, Beauty and the Beast embrace and live happily ever after.

This lovely fable, which has been made into a popular TV series, is a powerful metaphor of the frightening inner journey each of us must take throughout our lives. When we recognize the necessity, and summon up the will and the courage to confront and experience the most terrifying "monster" in our lives—our own hidden fears—we discover a depth of compassion and beauty within ourselves. In embracing fear and that which covers it, we find the love of our lives.

FEAR INVENTORY

Quickly, without mulling over your answers, circle the felt response, remembering that answers are neither right nor wrong, good nor bad. The truth, no matter how disappointing, is always preferable to self-delusion.

WHAT DO I FEAR

1.	I'm afraid to admit that I'm afraid.	T	F
2.	I'm afraid of losing control.	T	F
3.	I'm afraid of looking bad.	T	F
4.	I'm afraid of disappointing others.	T	F
5.	I'm afraid of losing someone I love.	T	F
6.	I'm afraid of sex.	T	F
7.	I'm afraid of spending my life alone.	T	F
8.	I'm afraid that my life has no purpose.	T	F
9.	I'm afraid of people who look strange.	T	F
10.	I'm afraid of taking risks.	T	F
11.	I'm afraid of making a fool of myself.	T	F
12.	I'm afraid of responsibility.	T	F
13.	I'm afraid that my life has no meaning.	T	F
14.	I'm afraid of strangers.	T	F
15.	I'm afraid of sticking my neck out.	T	F
16.	I'm afraid to tell the truth.	T	F
17.	I'm afraid of being controlled.	T	F
18.	I'm afraid of things I don't understand.	T	F
19.	I'm afraid of suffering.	T	F
20.	I'm afraid of death.	T	F
21.	I'm afraid of dying.	T	F
22.	I'm afraid of dying alone.	T	F

Look over your list. Do certain fears stand out for you?

TUNING INTO INTERPERSONAL FEARS

The following are some of the more common fears associated with intimacy.

- Losing oneself—giving up personal identity in exchange for being loved.
- Not being lovable, acceptable, or good—or good enough.
- Loss of control—not being in charge of myself and/or my life.
- Rejection and abandonment.

INTERPERSONAL FEARS QUIZ

1. I feel _____when I'm not in control in a relationship.
2. I feel enraged in a relationship when _____.
3. The prospect of rejection makes me feel _____.
4. I feel _____at the thought of not being perceived as "good enough" in a relationship.
5. The thought of losing control makes me feel _____.
6. I feel defensive in relationships when _____.
7. I feel _____when I experience a loss of identity in a relationship.
8. I feel _____at the prospect of not being perceived as lovable.
9. When I feel controlled in a relationship I feel _____.
10. I feel _____at the thought of being abandoned.
11. I feel frightened in a relationship when _____.
12. I feel hopeless and helpless in a relationship when _____.

OVERCOMING THE FEAR OF INTENSITY

You can do the following exercise with a partner or by yourself in front of a mirror.

1. Begin by repeating over and over either the word "Yes" or the word "No": No! No! No! or, Yes! Yes! Yes!
2. Start by speaking softly but allow your voice to grow louder and louder and louder!!
3. Now switch words and repeat the above.

FOLLOWING FEAR TO ITS NATURAL CONCLUSION

The following exercise starts out seriously but often ends by dissolving into giggles. As we push the edges of our fears we often discover how groundless or ludicrous many of them are.

1. Make a list of fears that you have.
2. Now, take one fear at a time and pretend that it has come true, see what happens by continuing to ask over and over and over again: "and now what?" For example:

If my fear is about losing control of my bodily functions, I would say, "I've lost control . . . and now what?" . . . "I'm disgusting." . . . "And now what?" "Nobody loves me." . . . "And now what?" "I'm just a big loathsome blob!" . . . "You know, I think I've heard that critical voice before many times."

After you have answered, "And now what." for the first

time, keep going. Ask it again and again and again until you reach a point where you gain some insight or the whole thing becomes funny.

LEARNING FROM NIGHTMARES

These are exercises that focus on fear.

1. As soon as you awake from a nightmare record the dream, though your wish may be to forget about it.
2. Relax yourself by breathing deeply, and pick up the dream at the point where it ended.
   - This is best done with your eyes closed, lying down.
   - If the dream has been particularly frightening, you may want someone close by to listen as you work with the dream.
3. If the dream was about falling, for example, fall to the point where you hit bottom and see what you find. If the dream ends as you're about to open a coffin, open it and look inside! What do you see?

People discover sources of fear by exploring nightmares. One nightmare understood is probably worth a year of conventional therapy! The same process applies to dreams that may not be nightmares but feel unfinished and incomplete. Return to the dream and complete it as a fantasy or daydream. The following dream changed the dreamer's life to such an extent that, after she completed the dreamwork, she experienced herself as more forceful in an ongoing way.

"I dreamed that there were two enormous but perfectly harmless snakes contained within a glass room. They meant me no harm, but their size, and the fact that they were snakes, repulsed me. I awoke feeling very disgruntled and it took time for me to build up the courage to do what I knew I must, which was to enter the room with the snakes. The process of concluding the dream in my waking state halted several times even though I was fully conscious. Finally, I entered the room and first touched, then embraced the huge creatures. At that point, I understood that the dream was calling my attention to my need to embrace the considerable strength within me, a strength that I had felt was appropriate only for a man."

By completing the dream as a fantasy she was able to accept and integrate an important aspect of her personality.

FACING THE FEAR OF DEATH

The following exercise is one I use to help people become aware that they are less afraid of death than they imagine. Most of us are more fearful of such things as suffering before death, or wasting our lives, than we are of death itself.

1. Make yourself comfortable in a setting where you will not be disturbed. Begin by relaxing parts of your body that may feel tight or uncomfortable. Take a few full, deep breaths.
2. Imagine that you are attending your own funeral. Create as vivid an image as you can. See, smell, hear, taste, touch, and feel what is going on.
   • What is happening?
   • Who is there?
   • How does it feel to be lying in your casket? Take

plenty of time to observe the events and to notice how you feel.

3. Imagine that the funeral is over and your casket is being placed in the ground and covered with dirt. Remember, you're dead—you're not being buried alive.
   • What is it like to be dead?
   • Are parts of death pleasant?
   • How is death different from life?

As we grow in our capacity to observe and accept ourselves, we may become aware of mind sets that color almost every aspect of our lives. One of these is the assumption that the universe is basically unfriendly. If this happens to be an assumption of yours, remember that you probably had a pretty good reason for making it in the first place. Remember also that yours is by no means a universal view, and that by accepting what you find to be true for yourself now, you can begin to enlarge your sense of possibilities.

CHAPTER 7

The Living Beyond Fear Process: Ride The Wild Horse

> *"All of us collect fortunes when we are children—
> a fortune of colors, of lights and darkness,
> of movements, of tensions. Some of us have
> the fantastic chance to go back to our fortune
> when we grow up."*
> —Ingmar Bergman

So far we have been following a path of self-observation that has stretched our understanding, compassion, and awareness of ourselves. Although little may seem to have outwardly changed, we are a little freer. In the years since our deepest fears took hold, we all have added enormously to our stockpile of personal resources. In addition to feeling, we are also intellect, will, and intuition. Since our youth, when we began to limit ourselves by anesthetizing our physical and emotional selves, we have been given repeated opportunities to reverse this pattern whenever those same feelings surfaced. If we could not have handled our feelings in the past, we can now, though the intensity of feeling may still be frightening. We will not die; we will not go mad. Healing and revitalization are at hand.

THE PURPOSE BEHIND THE PROCESS

We are now at a point in the process of self-exploration where the going gets tougher. The difference between mentally processing a feeling and experiencing that feeling is vast and often terrifying. The real solution lies in our capacity to fully experience the very emotions we have been protecting ourselves from. This is the purpose of the Living Beyond Fear process. It is through this raw experience of feeling that resolution and freedom can be attained.

The process you are about to be introduced to is one that will enable you to safely experience the most frightening of feelings. Once you have internalized it and made it yours, you will find it a resource for all times and all seasons. The process will ground and energize you. It will also clear your mind and enable you to be more genuinely loving toward yourself and others. By connecting mind and body, doors open to resources that enable us to face and overcome adversity.

SETTING THE STAGE

The environment in which you choose to work with your process is an important consideration. It should be comfortable, well ventilated, and quiet enough to offer no obvious distractions. You will be surprised at the number of possibilities that exist: a favorite room, the yard, the park, even a friend's home if necessary. I know one woman who gives her children to her husband and locks herself in the bathroom. Though it is not necessarily the most aesthetic environment, she laughingly admits there is no phone, and in her family, "the john is inviolate."

You might close the door to your office when the rest of the staff is out to lunch, or, as in the case of one very determined young woman, sit in your car. When there is intention, there is solution! It is vitally important that you also find a time when you are not tired or preoccupied, and when you will not be interrupted. You may have to experiment to find the best time or times for yourself, but I strongly urge you to find it and keep it.

Learning something new will require discipline on your part, for one doesn't sit down at the piano for the first time and play Chopin or the Beatles. The process takes skill to do well, and skill is built through repetition. If you spend some time practicing daily you will learn the process within six to twelve weeks. If you practice only now and then, you may never learn it.

THE PROCESS IS A FORM OF MEDITATION

The LIVING BEYOND FEAR (LBF) process is, for the most part, a meditation. It is, in fact, rather like Tibetan sitting meditation. If you already meditate, you understand that meditation is simply a process of giving full and undivided attention to a single point of reference. This focus might be directed toward a sound, as is the case with a mantra; it might be concentrating on the flicker of a flame, or on the sight of a flower, or on a feeling sensation. Our attention is usually so scattered and distracted by interruptions, that focus on any point of concentration can serve to narrow our attention and produce an altered state of consciousness. The LIVING BEYOND FEAR process helps us focus on the place in our body that houses the most "feeling intensity." Unless we have a headache, this point will be located somewhere *below* the bridge of the nose.

THE LIVING BEYOND FEAR PROCESS— RIDE THE WILD HORSE

PREPARATION

Prepare yourself for RIDE THE WILD HORSE by creating as safe and comfortable an environment as you possibly can. The following points should help you make the most of your time and energy:

- Take off your shoes and loosen your clothing.
- Take the phone off the hook, lock the door if necessary. You might even wish to hang up a "Do Not Disturb" sign.
- Select a chair or bed you find most comfortable. Some people prefer lying on a carpeted floor. If you have a tendency to fall asleep *don't* lie down. A comfortable straight-back chair will serve you best.
- Set a timer or alarm if you think you will be watching the clock. You should continue the process no more than sixty minutes nor less than a total of twenty minutes. You may wish to break up your time into smaller segments of perhaps ten minutes each. This is a *time-limited exercise*. Too much time can result in your not fully applying yourself, whereas giving yourself too little time can make you feel tense and incomplete.
- Stretch and move around before and after the exercise. Movement is especially helpful in releasing the muscular discomfort that often accompanies intense feelings.
- Please do not smoke, drink, or use any drugs (except those your doctor has specifically prescribed) before or

during the session. Please do not eat a large meal just before you begin, it will probably make you sleepy. And, of course, do not eat during the hour.

- Because of the importance of learning that you can continue on with whatever you are doing while you also perceive your feelings, I do not advise doing the exercise before bedtime.

INSTRUCTIONS

1. *Clear your mind of all extraneous thoughts.* Take several slow, deep breaths, releasing your thoughts with each exhalation. Make sure that you let go of as much air as you inhaled, otherwise you might feel lightheaded. Put one hand on your chest and the other on your belly. Are both hands moving? If they both are, you are breathing fully and deeply. If they are not, breathe in a little more fully and let go a little more completely. As you continue, allow your body to sink comfortably into the chair, bed, or floor. You might wish to deepen your breathing by repeating the words "soft belly" and "soft chest" as you breathe in and out.

2. *Identify an intense emotion/feeling or a situation to which you reacted with inappropriate intensity or significant physical or emotional discomfort.* If you are feeling emotionally agitated about something, use this feeling as your seed meditation. If you are not feeling particularly charged about anything, you can recall a recent emotional experience or a situation in which you reacted with inappropriate intensity. Perhaps you experienced significant physical/emotional discom-

fort in some unthreatening situation or for no apparent
reason.

3. *Re-create this moment as vividly as you can.* Touch,
taste, and smell the situation as well as hear and see
it in your mind's eye. As you allow yourself to go
more deeply into your experience, you can begin to
recall painful and difficult events or feelings connected to your memories.

4. *Continue to breathe fully and deeply and begin to scan
your body until you locate one part that stands out as
feeling more intense than other parts.* Do not be concerned if you find tension where you least expected it.
Once you locate it, direct your full attention toward
the feeling sensation. Experience it, breathe into its
center, and stay focused on this sensation!

5. *If your attention wanders, refocus on the intense feeling in your body.* Your attention will undoubtedly
wander away frequently to unrelated thoughts and images. Each time this happens, gently bring your attention back with your breath and refocus on the physical/
emotional feeling stored in your body. This may require you to momentarily "think": "I have lost
my focus." Don't waste time in self-recrimination—
simply redirect your focused attention back to the part
of your body where you are experiencing the greatest
"feeling intensity." If you feel nothing, focus on the
experience of emptiness. That's a feeling, too!

PERMITTING ALL THAT'S THERE TO SURFACE

6. *Allow the intensity of your feeling to grow.* Continue to breathe deeply, allowing the intensity to grow. Permit yourself to be frightened, angry, or sad, if that is how you feel. You may find it helpful to intensify the feeling by repeating, "I allow this feeling," on each inhalation and exhalation. If you choose to do this, don't dwell on this thought. Flash it as a momentary suggestion and just see what happens. The most important part of the process is the experience of physical and emotional sensation that takes place somewhere in your body. If your mind can't classify the feeling, that's okay—what's important is fully having the feeling.

If you begin with one emotion but find that it shifts or dissolves into another, or if the source of the feeling moves to another area of your body, permit this to happen, provided the shift intensifies your feeling sensations. *Follow the intensity, allowing it to be experienced fully, allowing it to intensify.* Feelings can transform in an instant: Rage can become sadness; sadness can give way to pain; grief can dissolve into rage. Any and all can transform into fear. Follow the feeling wherever it goes.

An image that I especially like is that of riding a wild horse. Your feeling, like the bucking, rearing horse, is full of fear and unbridled energy. The only way to tame it is to stay with it, to prove to it that it will not be hurt and that you will not be thrown off.

7. *Once a feeling has intensified, attempt to stay with it for ten to twenty minutes.* If feeling is an especially frightening experience for you, 2–5 minutes may be

what's appropriate for you to begin with. If this is the case, do the process several times for short periods during the day.

8. *Dialogue with your "feeling."* After "staying with your feeling," you may further get in touch with your feelings by directing questions to the feeling source in your body, not your mind. These questions are also appropriate to ask while you are doing the process, *provided that they don't distract you.*

• Are you a new feeling?
• If not, when did I first feel you?
• Do I feel you often?
• What do you have to teach me about myself?
• What is the feeling I am experiencing? Is it rage? Sadness? Fear? Is it the despair of numbing?

If an answer does not surface, do not be concerned. It is far more important to feel your feelings than to categorize them. You may wish to deepen your understanding by continuing to ask questions: "If I am sad, why am I sad, and why does that make me sad?" "If I'm angry, why am I angry, and why does that make me angry?" This kind of uncritical, gentle probing will eventually reveal hidden fear. Typically, we are most afraid of what could be or of what might happen related to the impressions and understanding we had as children. Questions like these can elicit intuitive responses that reveal in a moment what you may have missed recognizing for years.

9. *Experience the release of your previously blocked feeling.* Tears may flow; you may groan, cry out, speak, or wail, but not necessarily so. *One can also process within at a very deep level, quietly.* Some-

times, as you approach an intense feeling, you may go numb. If this is your experience, then let the feeling of non-feeling become your focus. Keep in mind that it is perfectly okay to feel frightened. The feeling of fear will never kill you or cause you to go mad because you have the capacity to direct your emotions appropriately. Feelings experienced in this manner bring about a greater measure of control.

10. *Monitor your energy level.* Progress with RIDE THE WILD HORSE is measured in terms of enhanced energy. A release of an old block may take several hours, or even days, to complete. The analogy here is that of a slow-draining wound. The more that is released, the more energy you will experience and the better you feel. This process is designed to initiate the opening of the block, and stored energy will continue to be released until you feel comfortable, equalized, and positively energized.

11. *Hold the feeling but not the thoughts.* Ending your experience is one of the most important parts of this process. When your time is up, stop exclusively focusing on your feelings and redirect your attention toward your routine activities. Though you are no longer giving your undivided attention to your physical and emotional feelings, it is important to retain some awareness of the sensations you just experienced. *Don't think about them*—feel them in your body. It is vital for you to learn that you can both continue to feel and at the same time focus your thoughts on other matters: your work, your family, and so on.

12. *When your time is up, pause for two or three minutes, breathing slowly and rhythmically, and relax.* You will notice your mind busying itself again. After this pause, get up and go about your day, allowing the physical/

emotional feelings you have uncovered to remain with you.

To summarize:

- Create an environment of comfort and safety.
- Clear your mind and concentrate on breathing fully and deeply.
- Relax your body.
- Take a moment to be aware of an emotional charge that you are carrying now or have carried in the past. Or, you may recall a recent experience in which you reacted with inappropriate intensity. Scan your body and observe which part houses the most "feeling intensity" when you recall this experience.
- Focus fully on this area and direct your breath to it.
- Ride the experience for as long as you can—up to ten or twenty minutes.
- Deepen with questions, which will reveal the source of the feeling if this is not distracting.
- End the exercise by shifting your focus from one of exclusive focus on feeling experience to one that also includes attention to other things.

The more you work with RIDE THE WILD HORSE, either on audio cassette or through your own practice, the less time you will need to locate and intensify your feelings. Eventually, you will be confident enough to permit intense feelings to be experienced fully at any time, secure in the knowledge that you can respond appropriately to them.

The intensity that may be evoked while doing this process is the result of tapping into emotions and energies that may have been trapped for many years. By staying calm in the face of emotional intensity, by breathing steadily while experiencing the physical sensation of the feeling, by acknowledging your emotions, you can ride your wild horse, staying in the saddle of your emotions, constructively using the energy and vitality and the will to be released. As long as you can continue to feel rather than think your feelings, you will stay safely astride, as the following stories exemplify.

Julie, a young psychologist, was one of the first people to make use of the LIVING BEYOND FEAR process. In the mid Seventies she sought me out at the advice of her physician because her diabetes was so out of control that she was frequently losing consciousness. Her physician feared that her blood sugar swings might be injuring her vital organs. Moreover, Julie had narrowly escaped being killed in an automobile accident as the result of a blackout a few months earlier.

Diabetes had been responsible for Julie's leading a protected life. She had been diagnosed at age seven, and from that time on she experienced herself as being different from other children. The fact that her father was a physician and her mother a nurse served to deepen her impression of being "at risk." Her family reinforced a pattern of dependency that she later brought to her marriage with Phil.

At Phil's insistence, and against her will, Julie accompanied him when he joined one of the controversial communes that was popular in the Seventies. This group demanded strict conformity from its members, and Julie bristled daily under a regime that she perceived as authoritarian. Their lives centered around the dictates of the group's dogmatic leader. At one point all couples were instructed to renounce their vow of fidelity, and to underscore this point, each person was given a separate bedroom. Phil complied in spite of Julie's fervent opposition. She repeatedly begged Phil to leave, but he refused. Julie hated the arrangement and was miserable but stayed nevertheless. She knew that the stress of the situation was contributing to her health problems but lacked the courage to leave.

As a professional, Julie was perfectly aware of the psychological dynamics of her situation. She knew that her health depended on her ability to sever her ties with the group. Also, she was aware that this probably meant severing her ties with Phil as well, but knowing this didn't affect her ability to change anything.

Julie eased into the LIVING BEYOND FEAR process carefully. While she knew a great deal about emotions and, in fact, had thought of herself as an emotional person, the process seemed scary at first. She had no trouble thinking about emotions, crying loud and long, or cursing, but when she had to pair these activities with a feeling focus somewhere in her body she felt overwhelmed. Understandably, she was also very sensitive to being told what to do and so she proceeded slowly at her own pace until she felt comfortable. While Julie was progressing with the process, her diabetes stabilized, and this encouraged her to press on.

Within six months she was able to connect with the depth of childlike fear and insecurity that had been a part of her life for as long as she could remember. Each day for a time-limited period she focused exclusively on these feelings. The rest of the time she allowed her emotions to remain with her as a "felt sense" in her body although she gave her primary attention to the tasks at hand. Julie used the LBF process to energize herself, and within six months, with the help of friends, she was able to move out of the commune and leave Phil.

I haven't seen Julie in years, but she sent me two announcements—one when she remarried, and another when her son was born. Both cards included notes that told me she was physically well and had thoroughly integrated the LBF process into her life. She had taught the process to her new husband and was using it with her clients.

Walt was a charming and handsome young attorney in his late twenties who was drawn to therapy in order to improve his relationships with women. He had been through a string of romances, all of which had ended unhappily. As we got to know one another, Walt confided that for many years he had suffered from colitis but that the problem was currently under control.

I had been seeing Walt for about two months when he came in white-faced one day and told me that he had just been diagnosed as having cancer of the lower intestine. Before the diagnosis, Walt had refused to practice the LIVING BEYOND FEAR process on his own. He had a million and one good reasons to explain why he never found the time to focus on his feelings. Most of these came down to an unwillingness to give up intellectual control and experience the vulnerable and insecure little boy part of himself. This was a part that he feared and disapproved of, but his illness as well as his behavior toward women underscored the urgency of his need to affirm his vulnerability.

In the face of his need for radical but life-saving surgery, Walt gave way to the fears he had tried so long and hard to stuff. The LIVING BEYOND FEAR process became a lifeline to the parts of himself that he needed to know in order to face what was ahead for him. He used the process to prepare himself for the surgery by focusing on all the feelings associated with losing a part of his body, and for carrying a bag around for the rest of his life. Walt also used the process to support his recovery and made every effort to stay with the experience of his feelings, below the bridge of the nose, and to avoid intellectualizing.

Many of Walt's fears had centered around remaining attractive to women. He was a young, unmarried man and wanted a wife and family. "Will anyone I find appealing, find me attractive?" he questioned. In the context of learning to experience his emotions, Walt made a delightful discovery. Not only did women continue to be interested in him, but they now seemed to find him more attractive than they had in the past. The perfection that he had believed was so important had in fact been a liability. Walt also discovered that in spite of what had happened to him, he felt more rather than less self-respect. Within a year of his surgery, Walt met and later married Kathy and they now have a baby daughter.

Walt stopped practicing the LBF process daily once he had fully recovered and resumed his busy life. However, he tells me that whenever something is troubling him, he is immediately aware of it and once more sets aside a period of time every day to focus exclusively on his feelings. He does this until he once more feels physically clear and emotionally peaceful. Sometimes, of course, he discovers things that require him to take action. Most of the time, however, he simply experiences his feelings and finds that the process itself leaves him sufficiently centered and energized to continue on.

* * *

Ronda was an attractive middle-aged woman who began our first meeting by telling me that she was worried about a recurrence of cancer. Twelve years before, Ronda had successfully undergone surgery for a malignant tumor. Recently, however, she had begun to experience mysterious pain in her leg and hip. The X rays that had been taken had proved inconclusive, but she was afraid of becoming ill in the future. I asked Ronda to describe her life during the last twelve years and she told me the following:

Shortly before her diagnosis of cancer, she had divorced her husband, the father of her then two young children. She had been an alcoholic and drug abuser at this point in her life. The stress and abuse of her marriage had contributed to these addictions. Friends in A.A. had helped her see this and had supported her in divorcing her husband. Since this time she had faithfully adhered to the program and had continued to go to meetings at least once a week. Indeed, from that point on she had devoted herself to only two things: raising her children, and staying clean and sober.

Life had been simple and straightforward for a dozen years, but with her children now grown and out of the house she had finally come face to face with the fact that she needed more from life than she was getting. She had created a safe cocoon, but it wasn't fulfilling enough. Though witty, bright, and attractive, Ronda had not dated since the divorce nor had she advanced professionally. Her fear of men had limited her career options. She wasn't old enough to die but neither A.A. nor the good friends she had made there were enough to give her life the purpose and meaning she needed to go on living.

Ronda resisted learning the LIVING BEYOND FEAR

process. After all, she reasoned, she had no trouble "getting hysterical" as she put it. At the familiar A.A. meetings and with her grown children she routinely cried and got angry, but not with strangers—especially when they were men!

As Ronda began to use the LBF process, the depth of her fears surprised and shocked her. Her fear of men had begun with her father, who had frightened and humiliated her. Her feelings of terror were so early and so intense that she began to feel that she must have been molested by her father when she was very young. The more Ronda allowed herself to recall these feelings, bit by bit, the more she understood herself and the greater became her eagerness to reenter the mainstream of life. She quit the agency where she had worked for years as a temp and took a full-time position as administrative assistant to the male vice president of a large technical company. Here she met and interacted with dozens of new people, some of whom became good friends.

Ronda remains healthy and physically active. Her pain and the shadows on the X rays of her hip and leg have disappeared. Fear no longer operates at an unconscious level in her life as she uses the LBF process to cope appropriately with her new friendships and relationships.

EXCUSES HOLD US BACK

The people who stand to gain the most by using the LIVING BEYOND FEAR process often find excuses to avoid practicing it. For example, burned-out doctors, nurses, social workers, or other health-care professionals will say, "It's unprofessional to be emotional. I've been trained to put my feelings aside in order to function pro-

fessionally.'' ''I can't let young cancer or AIDS patients
see my fears, grief, or personal sense of loss; nor do I
dare let myself dwell on such feelings. I would lose it
professionally.'' Wrong! It simply is not the case that experiencing a ''felt sense'' of emotion within your body
inhibits professional behavior. Quite the contrary. It is the
process of pushing aside feelings that clouds our thinking
and inhibits our creativity. When we bog down emotionally, we also bog down intellectually. Moreover, patients
and loved ones appreciate and need to see that they do
touch us emotionally. This makes them feel less alone and
provides substantial comfort.

Remember, the LIVING BEYOND FEAR process
teaches us to contain emotional intensity—to process it by
staying with the physical experience in our bodies. The fear
that most people have of ''acting out'' is neutralized by this
process. We may choose to act, but by the time we do so,
our rational mind will be connected to our actions. Our
intellects are perfectly capable of seeing to it that behavior
is appropriate, provided we avoid becoming overwhelmed
and stay on top of our fears. It is precisely this ability to
ride our fears and thus be able to act appropriately that the
LIVING BEYOND FEAR process provides.

People who are ill also have concerns about becoming
overwhelmed. If this is the case for you, proceed at a
slower pace. Practice the process at first for only two or
three minutes at a time, so as to maintain your sense of
control. Once you trust the process, you will be able to
focus for a longer period. A very full release can be wonderful, but it can also feel overwhelming. Bigger releases
are not necessarily better releases. It is important that you
feel in control of the process in order to stay motivated.

Another question frequently asked is, ''How do I know

that I have worked with the process long enough?'' Here, the answer is simple and dependable. Any release will immediately effect an increase in energy. If you feel drained or headachy after practicing, you have *not* done it. Instead, you are once again blocking your emotions.

HOW MUCH TIME DO I NEED TO GIVE THE PROCESS?

''How long do I continue practicing the process?'' That depends on your needs. As I said, you can probably learn the technique within six to twelve weeks of almost daily practice. Once you have it down pat, the process belongs to you and you can integrate it whenever you are in an emotionally charged situation. If you are attempting to release deep emotional blocks as a part of a healing process, you will want to continue focusing daily until you feel absolutely clear of emotional glitches in almost any context. Sometimes a ''thorough housecleaning'' takes months or even years. For example, blocks that were created because of experiences that involved childhood incest or abuse can be deeply buried. If, however, you patiently continue to work with the process, the feelings that surround these memories will eventually surface.

''What if I don't feel anything, and I've been doing the process every day for a week?'' What this means is that you have been practicing ''not feeling'' for years. Stay with your focus on the feeling of emptiness, numbness, or nothingness that you *do* feel. Within a few weeks or less you will be able to identify feeling sensations.

''Can I use the process to focus on 'good' feelings?'' Of course. Just remember that sometimes ''feeling good'' is scary—especially if you are not used to feelings of well-being. Take it slowly if you need to—but keep going.

"YES, BUT . . ."

Finally, there are a group of questions that I categorize as, "Yes, buts." These are not really questions—they're justifications for not doing the process. Of course getting in touch with your emotions isn't easy. If it were, you would already be perfectly comfortable experiencing a full range of your most intense feelings.

Some days, of course, will be more productive than others. From time to time you will undoubtedly hit an area you don't want to deal with. When this happens, you will feel drained because you will have put effort into not knowing, even though you have gone through the motions. Once again your energy level, increased sensitivity, and heightened awareness will tell you that you are on target!

As you progress, a great many sensitive areas will be stressed. If you are like most people, you will do almost anything to escape feeling emotionally unsettled or uncomfortable. But the very act of avoiding pain is the same act that dulls everything in our lives that is also useful, positive, and constructive. Remind yourself again and again and again, if necessary, that you bought this book to learn. Although some of what you may be learning is not what you expected or even like, nonetheless, it is giving you options that you did not have before. The question should not be, "Does it hurt?" but rather, "Does it help me improve the quality of my life?" The discipline, responsibility, and commitment you build when you encourage yourself to face your fears will help you heal the very pain you dread.

In this culture, most people devote their reflective time to thinking. Rarely do they observe how they feel. They examine, brood, and worry about the past and the future, seldom spending a moment in the present to reach resolution or completion. Yet, growth, movement, and progress can take place only within the context of "this very moment."

When you feel like abandoning the whole process or wish you had never found this book, know for sure that you are making enormous strides. The stronger your resistance, the closer you're coming to the truth. Stay with it. Stay with yourself. No one ever died or went mad from the truth, only from the repression and anxiety of the constant denial of their feelings.

When all else fails, give yourself permission to "stop trying so hard." Take a break. Spend a day in bed or at the beach, take a long walk in a beautiful setting. Go to a movie in the afternoon when you think you should be working, buy yourself a present, reward yourself in some creative, if not occasionally extravagant, way. Do something totally self-indulgent! Let the child within you play. Sometimes *doing less* in a conscious and focused way results in renewed energy, inspiration, and enthusiasm.

Above all, do not forget you have a sense of humor, even if it has been forced into dormancy. Take a step back from yourself, from your situation, from your transformational goals. Try not to make change such a heavy business. Laugh at yourself occasionally. You may grow to enjoy it!

From here on I recommend that you use the LIVING BEYOND FEAR process to illuminate and support all the quizzes and inventories that follow. LBF will do the same for any program or process that you choose to involve yourself with from now on.

PART IV

Deepening

CHAPTER 8

Pain and Grief

"And a woman spoke, saying, 'Tell us of Pain.'
And he said:
'Your pain is the breaking of the shell that encloses
your understanding.' "
—*Kahlil Gibran*

PAIN SERVES A PURPOSE

The function of pain is to sustain and protect life. Its shrill alarm alerts us to danger. Pain, be it physical or emotional, is functional, purposeful, and must be acknowledged. We urgently need to take our hand off the stove, come in out of the cold, deal with injury, meet our needs, stop pushing love away, and allow our divided selves to be integrated. Pain is the signal to take notice, to wake up, to act, to open; and the way we tend to react to pain can reveal hidden assumptions and beliefs about ourselves.

Chronic emotional pain and suffering are generated by the belief that something essential and irreplaceable has been hopelessly lost. "I will never attain the life I want." "I will never get another chance like that." "I have lost the best job I will ever have." "I will never love again." "My best friend, support, love, or purpose in life is gone." Devastated, deeply depressed, the people who feel this way believe they are absolutely alone and have lost

151

their dreams, their goals, their hopes. Or, as Stephen Levine so aptly put it in *A Gradual Awakening*, "Wanting things to be otherwise is the very essence of suffering."

PAIN CAN BE DISGUISED

Emotional pain, like all feelings, can be pushed from conscious awareness or converted into more "tolerable" emotions. The vulnerability we feel as the result of pain, can be transformed into rage, masked with humor, or deadened with food, alcohol, drugs, or compulsive behaviors; but it cannot ever be completely shut out. To some degree, emotional and physical pain will always be with us when we feel hurt. Individuals generally experience a greater degree of either physical or emotional pain. The familial patterns determining the likeliness of one form of pain over the other tend to be handed down from one generation to another.

PAIN CARRIES AN IMPORTANT MESSAGE

Pain is deadened but not resolved in a society that consumes thousands of pounds of aspirin daily. The tranquilizers, mood elevators, and muscle relaxants used to calm emotional pain are among the top prescription drugs in this country. Pain of any type frightens us, and our resistance to it is a mental and physical tightening that actually magnifies it. But pain is our teacher—a ferocious one, but our teacher nonetheless.

Physical pain, signaling the breakdown of homeostasis, which maintains the subtle balance of life in the body, can come as a reaction to injury or disease, and can follow on the heels of emotional suffering. Intense or chronic pain, particularly that which cannot be justified or explained through physical causes, has long been a puzzlement to medical science, since it appears to lack biological purpose. There is just "no physical explanation for it." Today, successful work with chronic pain has come about through a psychological focus. Chronic pain patients are asked to consider the fact that their pain may be a way of not dealing with their lives or a substitute for emotions they want to ignore.

We, of course, have all used pain as an excuse for nonaction—"I can't go to the party tonight, I don't feel well enough." "Can I stay home from school today, Mom? I feel sick. I can take the test tomorrow." "Not tonight, dear, I have a headache." Long-time sufferers are asked to reflect on their responses to such questions as, "What message about my life does this pain convey?" "What lesson do I need to learn?" "What am I afraid to do that is important to me?" "What am I hiding from?" The root cause of their suffering often runs into their worst fear and dread. But the wisdom of this approach to pain in regard to relentless physical as well as emotional suffering was dramatically revealed to me early in my work with cancer patients.

Eddie, a very loving and protective man in his early forties, was dying of cancer of the lymphatic system. He had put up a truly courageous fight for several years but had finally grown weary. Leaving the hospital, he returned home to die.

Eddie had carefully examined and radically improved many areas of his life. Although his relationships with friends and family had blossomed, he had been unable to alter his relationship with his wife, Ann. He loved her deeply and she him, but the specter of death and her un-willingness to confront her grief and fear lay like a deep and bridgeless gap between them. I, too, tried many times to engage Ann in conversation about her husband, but she simply refused to speak about him with me or anyone. I understood how deeply she was suffering and hoped that sooner or later she would reach out for the help and support she so desperately needed.

One afternoon shortly after Eddie left the hospital, I received a frantic call from Ann. Eddie was in such agony that he could neither sit nor lie down. All he could do was pace the floor, moaning and crying. Everything medically possible to alleviate the pain had been done. The nerve endings connected to the areas in his throat and shoulder, which were the source of his suffering had been severed. Yet the pain intensified. Even the strongest opiates produced little relief.

I had absolutely no idea how to improve the situation, but I too loved Eddie and so set out on the long drive to his home, praying all the way for guidance. I arrived just as he dozed off for the first time in days. Later, it occurred to me that perhaps he had fallen asleep when he heard my car pull into the driveway, knowing that what he needed would somehow, some way, be taken care of.

I found myself alone with Ann in the kitchen. On a hunch, I asked her once again if she would be willing to speak openly to her husband about her fears and concerns, and to listen to his as well. "All of them?" she asked hesitantly. "All," I replied, "including the fact that Eddie is likely to die soon." She paused for several moments and then in a clear, strong voice replied, "I'll do anything that would ease my husband's suffering."

Eddie awoke at that moment, as if he had heard her

statement, and called us to come to him. Tears filled my eyes as I witnessed what was surely a triumph of love over fear. For the next several hours the three of us explored with great thoroughness every concern, every emotion, every uncertainty, every fear either of them had about dying, death, and what would come after, how she would manage, the children, his parents. They also shared the joy and gratitude they felt in having known and loved each other. To this day I consider those few hours among the most beautiful and relevant in my life.

After that conversation, Eddie's pain abruptly came to an end. He died a few days later in perfect peace, surrounded by people he loved. His head was cradled in his father's hands, Ann's hands were in his, over his heart. Eddie's agony had been a message that he profoundly needed to convey his thoughts and feelings to his wife, to feel her acceptance, her strength, and her love. Unfortunately, his pain had to assume agonizing proportions; yet, without it, he never would have had the opportunity to resolve the conflict with his wife, which then led to so tranquil a death.

FEAR MAKES PAIN HURT MORE

Eddie's story also points to the fact that much of what we experience as pain is anxiety or dread of the future. People sometimes find themselves in the convoluted situation of being in pain because they fear the future holds even more pain.

When my son was little, he would agonize for hours before his appointment with the pediatrician for his shots. Once in the office, he made life such hell for all concerned that it usually took two hefty nurses to hold him still long enough for the doctor to prick him with the needle. Afterward, he was fine, but I went home and took to my bed with two aspirin and a cold cloth.

His younger sister was not any fonder of shots, but she responded quite differently. Even as a toddler, she would march into the doctor's office, stick out her arm, shriek once at the top of her voice when the needle was inserted, and then happily continue with the rest of the examination.

Clearly, the amount of suffering my son endured was far greater than that of his sister. Her pain had to do with being pricked physically, and it was over in a blink of an eye. His pain was based on memories of similar past experiences—pain that sprang from terrified expectations of the future and that lasted for hours. It always turned out as badly as he imagined it would.

Most people's pain results from the consequence of their struggle against the experience, not the experience itself. So often the worst part about any unpleasant, unavoidable event is the anticipation or expectation of what will happen. Because we feel tense and anxious, we tighten and constrain our bodies in ways that in themselves produce pain and suffering. In situations where we cannot run, cannot fight, and will not surrender to the experience, we often resist in ways that ensure an experience of what we dread most.

You're probably asking, "So what?" The problem may have been ably diagnosed, but how do you handle the agony once you're in the midst of it? To simply tell someone that his or her pain is psychosomatic does not in any way diminish it.

By now you might have guessed that my recommendation for appropriately treating pain is the same as my recommendation for treating all intense feelings: Face it, go into it; experience it; and the process will set you free.

David, a sensitive young man in his twenties, introduced himself to me with this statement: "If I can't get some relief from this pain, I'm going to kill myself." For over a year and a half he had lived day in and day out with unrelentingly severe pelvic pain, which began as a result of a severe infection in his groin. The infection had healed, yet his suffering had continued. His pain had been unsuccessfully treated medically and could be neither explained nor understood. David had consulted with a number of competent doctors, all of whom assured him that the pain was due to his nerves. He was given tranquilizers and muscle relaxants, which made him sleepy but did not reduce his distress.

When he came to me, I asked him to consider what he thought about most of the time. His response was "tomorrow's pain, and pain the day after, and the day after that." He actually spent most of his time fearing pain that was "coming." I suggested that he try the LIVING BEYOND FEAR process. I recommended that he create a safe, private, comfortable environment; that he relax himself with the breathing technique, and then focus on the very center and most intense part of his pain. For twenty minutes daily, without thinking about or analyzing anything, he just experienced the feeling in his groin. If or when the pain recurred, he repeated the exercise.

David found that when he stopped thinking about his suffering in a past or future context and, instead, directed his attention to the sensation itself, the pain diminished to a point where it was bearable.

This victory was not the end for David; it was only the

beginning. As a consequence of living in the moment, he began facing the many important issues in his life that he had been avoiding. He continues to face them, and he continues to be free of this particular pain. What David did in focusing on his pain was to open himself up to the understanding that it was not only the pain in his body that he had resisted; it was also the self-doubt, the self-criticism, and the fear that had imprisoned him.

GRIEF

Grief is perhaps the most painful of emotions to bear. One feels an emptiness, a hollowness, a longing that borders on sickness. We have all experienced this to some degree. It is not only an emotion felt at the loss of a loved one, but also the deep desire for life to be different from the way it is.

Grief may be difficult, but it is absolutely necessary. We cannot let go, forgive, or heal emotionally unless we grieve first. But the question we face is, "How do we grieve?" How, indeed, do we express grief in a society that ignores dying and death? How can we experience the magnitude of our sorrow and loss when to do so implies that we are being self-indulgent? How is one to respond to such well intended remarks as, "It's all for the best." "They were suffering anyway." "They're happier because they are with God now."

I remember a young woman who took me aside at a center intended to offer support to the families of dying children. She said, "It's been over six months since I lost my baby and I'm still grieving. What's wrong with me?"

What's wrong with a culture that makes a mother feel guilty for missing her only child? We don't have to be ashamed of our grief. It is real; it is about loss. And unless we acknowledge this loss, our attempts at letting go, forgiving, and renewal will be aborted or stunted.

AIDS has added a new dimension to grief for millions of Americans. The loss of a loved one is always tragic—this is especially true when the person who died is young. However, the gay community has had to confront not only the loss of many friends and beloveds but also a life-style. As one man in a group put it, "This is a holocaust: I have lost my druggist, dentist, and clothier. When will my turn come?"

Unfortunately, we have few rituals for acknowledging and resolving grief. Most funerals are showplaces with the dead painted so prettily that they look far better in their caskets than they did when they were alive.

Rituals surrounding death and dying are an integral part of many cultures, but they are not a part of ours. And yet they should be. The "quilt" is an example of a ritual created by the gay community in order to grieve publicly for those who have died. It is made up of hundreds, perhaps thousands at this point, of squares, each commemorating the life of an individual who has died of AIDS. Many more such rituals need to be created in order for people to routinely grieve both privately and publicly.

Grief is also an ongoing element in the lives of those who specialize in caring for dying individuals. Doctors, nurses, social workers, hospice personnel, and volunteers routinely experience grief as a part of their work. The only way to avoid a sense of loss is to push emotions so far into the background that one's capacity to be emotionally present is lost. When this is the case, not only are health-care professionals and volunteers less effective in their roles, but the satisfaction derived from helping others pales or disappears entirely. This contributes to stress and burn-out. There is no way that an emotionally present health-care provider can see patient after patient die—especially young ones—without being personally touched. Unfortunately, this fact is totally ignored in most schools of medicine and even in the fields of psychology and social work. There is little in the way of training that prepares one for the loss of patients.

One of the most cleansing and renewing experiences I have had was initiated when a group I belong to participated in a spontaneous grieving ritual. Several of our members had recently lost parents and we set aside an evening to focus on this fact. A large circle was formed and we began by inviting those who had recently experienced losses to enter the center and speak. A few of the more verbal members got up and came into the circle to tell their story of loss. Others joined them to speak, or to cry, or simply to identify silently with what had been said.

As the evening progressed, more and more people entered the circle. We had begun early in the evening, but because so many had so much grief to share, we continued late into the night. People spoke not only about the loss of parents but about the loss of other loved ones as well. In the context of love and acceptance created by the group of silent witnesses that formed the circle, people who had been unable to grieve for years were able to do so at last. Members of our group who were gay also had an opportunity to share their experience with AIDS.

Over the course of the evening many people entered the circle but no one left until everyone, without exception, had expressed their grief. At the conclusion of the ritual we were tired but also relaxed and very peaceful. It was easy to sleep soundly that evening. The following day, and from then on, an extraordinary air of intense energy and vitality ran through the group. Something very deep, cleansing, and truly wonderful had taken place.

HURT AND SADNESS EXPRESSED AS ANGER

Chronic hurt and sadness frequently surface as internalized rage or irrational anger directed toward others. The world is full of sad, outwardly kind individuals who in the flash of an eye can become aggressive belligerent bullies. Alcohol supports this process, but it can happen completely independently of alcohol or drugs. The tragedy here is that the people who get "dumped on" tend to be those who are closest to the individuals who are carrying the emotional pain. Families and coworkers—people they like, love, and need—are the ones they most hurt.

A young woman in a managerial position came to me to help her resolve "her problem with rage." In the work setting she would frequently lash out uncontrollably at times and in ways that were as disturbing to her as the people she supervised. The LBF process made it clear that hurt and sadness, rather than rage, were her real issues. Hurt and sadness also contributed to a chronic skin condition that cleared up once she began addressing her real feelings.

One of the questions this client, and many in her situation, asked is "How much of this can I let go of?" How much hurt, pain, sadness, and grief can any of us let go of? The answer to this question is, "As much as we will allow." The more consistently we work with ourselves and the LBF process, the greater will be the release of emotional blocks, and the freer and more energized we will become. When we experience our sadness, our grief, our anger, our deepest fears, we are quite literally healing ourselves.

To live is to risk pain from time to time. Learning to experience pain appropriately does not remove it from our lives, but it does free us from protections that constrict and diminish the quality of our lives. Once we embrace our resistance to pain and grief, we discover a messenger that can direct us to paths of renewed energy, enthusiasm, compassion, and joy.

PAIN AND GRIEF INVENTORY

Answer the following questions by consulting your physical and emotional feelings. Again, there are no correct answers to any of the following questions, only points of departure.

Circle the answer that best describes how you feel.

1. I spend a lot of time in pain. T F
2. I'm rarely depressed. T F
3. My life is full of meaning and purpose. T F
4. I'm afraid that tomorrow won't be any better than today. T F
5. I rarely think about my losses. T F
6. I often talk about my aches and pains. T F
7. I expect life to be painful. T F
8. I never have felt grief. T F
9. I try to ignore my physical pains. T F
10. I never focus on anything that is negative. T F
11. I would rather not feel than feel bad. T F
12. When I hurt myself, I usually ignore it. T F

13. I frequently use sickness as an excuse.   T   F

14. I need drugs to ease my pain.   T   F

15. I suffer much more emotionally than physically.   T   F

16. My mother often complained of aches and pains.   T   F

17. I can't remember the last time I wasn't in pain.   T   F

18. I can always find some way to numb bodily pain.   T   F

19. I think suffering silently is noble.   T   F

20. I'm afraid to talk about my pain.   T   F

21. I fear being in pain more than anything.   T   F

22. Going to the dentist terrifies me.   T   F

23. I will do anything to avoid unpleasantness.   T   F

24. Men can withstand hardship better than women can.   T   F

25. I can't bear to be around anyone who is in pain.   T   F

26. I usually let my pain run its course naturally.   T   F

27. Strong people don't complain about their pain.   T   F

28. I believe pain has something to teach me.   T   F

29. Life is hard and full of pain.   T   F

30. When I'm in pain, I feel out of control.   T   F

31. I have never felt intense pain of any kind.   T   F

32. I use alcohol as a painkiller.   T   F

PAIN - HOW DO I KNOW THEE?

List five ways you control your physical pain.

List five ways you control your emotional discomfort.

List several experiences that have caused you grief.

List the ways in which you deal with grief.

Write your immediate response in the space provided using only one or two words.

PAIN BY OTHER NAMES

1. When I think about pain, I'm reminded of _____.
2. The physical pain of others makes me feel _____.
3. I feel grief most often in my _____.
4. The worst pain I can remember as a child was when I was _____ years old.
5. My family dealt with physical pain by _____.
6. The worst kind of pain is _____.
7. The worst thing about pain is that it makes me feel _____.
8. I feel pain most often in my _____ and my _____.
9. People who give in to their pain are _____.
10. I feel _____ when I am around people who are grieving.
11. The thing I fear most about pain is _____.
12. When I feel grief, I _____.
13. People who talk about their pain are _____.
14. The most intense physical pain I have ever felt was _____.
15. The most intense emotional pain I have ever felt was when _____.
16. I push my feelings of loss away by _____.
17. Women deal with pain by _____.
18. Men deal with pain by _____.
19. When I was a child, my family expressed grief by _____.
20. I feel comfortable sharing my grief with _____.
21. When I lose something of great value, I _____.

22. If I could change my life this moment, I would _____.

23. The physical excuse I usually use for nonaction is that I'm _____.

24. I would rather feel the emotion of _____than grief.

25. People hurt me the most by _____me.

EXPERIENCING GRIEF AND LOSS

Keep in mind that the point of the exercises that follow is to relieve you of the burdensome and limiting habit of investing a great deal of energy in not knowing and not feeling.

YOUR RELATIONSHIP TO LOSS

If you have reason to believe that grief or loss is an issue for you, spend at least several weeks on the following exercise:

1.(a). Begin the LBF process by posing the following question: "What have I lost?" Locate the spot in your body that produces a feeling response and focus on the experience of your feelings. If you need to, repeat the question in order to stay focused, but *don't think about the question*, rather briefly repeat, "What have I lost?" to yourself.

(b). Once you have become more intensely aware of your sense of loss, you will be ready to continue with the second part of this exercise, but not before! Do not attempt to resolve your grief until you have experienced it at a feeling level.

2. Repeat the LBF process, but this time go into it with the question, "What have I *not* lost?" or, "What have I learned, gained, etc."

3. Finally, you may wish to complete the process by considering how, as the result of this loss, you can improve your own life and the lives of others.

CREATIVE APPLICATIONS OF PAIN

1. If you are experiencing physical pain, itching, or some other intense bodily discomfort, direct your breath and attention to an ever-diminishing area of distress (the forearm, for instance). Visualize the area as a circle. Spend a minute or two breathing into the pain, focusing on it. Continuing on, try to locate the part of the circle of pain that is the most intense (perhaps just above the wrist). Again, continue breathing rhythmically and focus your attention on this area for a couple of minutes. Next, determine the center of this circle where the pain is most intense (try to visualize the spot where the pain seems to intensify) and go on breathing into it, experiencing this new point of discomfort. Keep your focus on this area for a few minutes. Continue in this way, focusing and breathing into each new center as each new single point decreases in circumference until the nucleus of the pain becomes so minute as to be impossible to visualize, and the point of discomfort diminishes or disappears entirely.

2. Experience the type of pain you are having (whether the cause is physical or emotional) by asking yourself the following questions while breathing fully and deeply. Open yourself to the feelings and sensations that will arise as you focus and breathe into them.

- What does the sensation of this pain feel like? Hot? Cold? Tearing? Aching? Dull? Cramping? Shrill?
- What is the quality of the sensation? Is it solid? Does it have weight? Color? Does it move around or stay in one place? Is it constant or intermittent? Is it round? Soft? Flat? Textured?
- Does the sensation seem to come from one point or are there several points?
- Are there many levels and sensations or only one? Do they vary in intensity?
- Does the sensation of the pain remind me of anything?

Continue breathing and focusing on your answers. Stay open to any pictures, sounds, colors, feelings, that come up for you. Let your body describe the sensations of pain to you.

3. There are times, as when someone you love has died or is slowly dying, that pain and grief seem interminable. Months or even years may pass as you stand by helplessly watching a loved one die of a terminal illness. Again, permitting yourself to experience your feelings of grief, anger, and helplessness will make it possible for you to cope with difficult situations. During the tough times when you feel like screaming, shouting, or crying hysterically, or when you feel you are going crazy, breathe steadily into the emotion by locating the place in your body that houses its greatest intensity. Focus and breathe, breathe and focus. If you feel, not think, about your emotions, you will find that even in the most chaotic of situations, your head will be clear, your heart will be open, and you will intuitively know how to behave.

4. If feelings of pain and grief linger without apparent cause, direct the following questions to the source of your feelings.

- Could these feelings be anger instead of grief?
- If they are, with whom am I angry? Acknowledge the answer that surfaces from your feeling self even if it happens to be someone who has died or is ill or disabled. Allow the feelings of anger at this person or event, however irrational they may seem, to intensify and be experienced.
- Could these feelings be fear instead of grief? If so, of what am I afraid? Accept whatever surfaces and direct your breathing to the source of the feelings you have uncovered.

CHAPTER 9

Rage

> *"The tigers of wrath are wiser*
> *than the horses of instruction."*
> —William Blake

As children many of us experienced rage as a tangible entity. Rage had a personality—a shape, size, color, texture, sound. Like a stray cat looking for a handout, it simply attached itself to us or to those we loved—too ugly and fierce to have been owned.

Rage is explosive, passionate, consuming. It is fury, momentary madness, anger gone berserk, the "urge to kill." Lying beneath its volcanic exterior are anger, outrage, grief, despair, and fear; it is the result of the actual or threatened denial of needs for safety, security, love. Infants turn fiery red and scream with rage when frightened or denied basic needs. As adults we fear its potential for destruction; we deny its demand for outlet. Yet rage is also the "fight" in the fight or flight response. It can inspire and empower us with both great physical strength and seemingly inexhaustible energy. Rage can save our lives as well as destroy them.

NEED AND DENIAL

Our feelings of rage were pushed into unconsciousness when we learned to hold our breath, clench our teeth, and squeeze our bodies to deaden the fierce emotion that surged upward in us toward the surface. We had to learn to prohibit anger in order to conform to society's definition of acceptable behavior. This was particularly true if the adults in our lives were volatile or abusive. Our natural feelings were swallowed as we were persuaded, manipulated, cajoled, or punished into "keeping quiet," in order to avoid frightening or enraging others. As a result, we became increasingly anesthetized to the very needs and feelings that triggered our rage in the first place.

Rage is kindled by the survival force itself, and therefore it will always be an integral part of life. If we continue to deny its presence, it festers and grows. With the addition of each new denial, each new assault, a last straw eventually drops onto our emotional pile and we erupt, often harming ourselves and others. Our furious outbursts come as blasts; tempers snap and we lash out, red-faced, shaking. We smash and throw things. We yell, swear, and fight. At other times we boil and seethe just below the surface, our heads pounding, our stomachs in knots, our teeth gnashing, and our bodies stiffening until, painfully, we confine our furies to our interior world.

The inner expression of rage hurts us, at times drastically. Ongoing suppressed rage is the basis of such illnesses as hypertension, colitis, stroke, bursitis, migraines, and chronic back pain. The outward expression of rage hurts others, sometimes pathetically, tragically; wife beating, child beating, the abuse of the elderly or the infirm, are grisly reminders of our potential for violence. Because of society's taboos, we often hold in our emotions during threatening situations and release them later once we feel safe. For example, should we fail to get the deserved recognition for our work, or worse yet, that praise was given to someone else, we would become resentful, angry. Rather than reveal our feelings to ourselves, much less publicly, we would push them inward, only to arrive home and vent our pain and frustration on our families.

INTERNALIZED RAGE

Perhaps the deadliest form of anger is internalized rage, the obsessive anger that is directed toward ourselves. Feelings of resentment, frustration, and self-loathing are created when we live in environments that repeatedly tell us we're "bad," "wrong," "no good." When these kinds of messages are communicated often enough we begin to believe them and repeat them to ourselves—again and again and again! Children and young people are especially vulnerable because they lack the means to defend themselves against the onslaughts of negativity that produce such internalized patterns. What is a child to do with such feelings—who will listen or understand? There is thus a level at which we may believe terrible things about ourselves, and doing so makes us understandably enraged. In the absence of hope or comfort, feelings are stuffed, silenced, and held within our bodies—perhaps for years.

In light of the messages that most homosexual youngsters get from parents, churches, and society in general it is not surprising that internalized homophobia is so common among gays. Members of minority groups also experience the pressure of enraging negative messages. They, too, are likely to internalize this information unless it is counterbalanced by constructive communication from their families and communities.

Internalized rage is a serious health hazard. The process of dealing with anger by stuffing it is particularly hard on our bodies because anger is such a powerful emotion. It takes enormous amounts of energy to bury rage. Stress evoked by this process is intense and undermines both physical and emotional health.

THE RELATIONSHIP BETWEEN RAGE AND PAIN

Nancy was a quiet, restrained young woman who for many months had sought a medical solution to the chronic pain she experienced in her stomach. Though she had undergone extensive testing nothing of a physiological nature could be found.

Her physician had then prescribed tranquilizers for stress, but these only made her sleepy while failing to reduce her suffering. At the point of losing her accounting job, she reluctantly sought psychological help.

Nancy bristled at the thought of her pain being psychosomatic. However, when I explained that emotionally based pain was, in fact, real pain and not simply a figment of one's imagination, she relaxed.

Nancy told me that she had been raised by her grandparents after the death of her mother and father in an automobile accident. Her grandparents had been fearful and protective, rarely letting Nancy out of their sight. She recalled that throughout grade school her grandfather had insisted on walking her to and from the play yard every day, although their apartment was only a few short blocks from the school. She was also not allowed to exert herself and even as a teenager was required to lie down and rest frequently. Friendships, too, were difficult because her grandparents found the other children "rowdy." All of this served to isolate Nancy but she assured me that she really had not minded her grandparents' intervention. They had been kind and attentive and she had never lacked for anything. She loved them dearly and missed them terribly since their death.

When Nancy first began working with the LBF process she experienced only deep sadness over the loss of her parents and grandparents, but within a short time feelings of anger and resentment began to displace those of grief. Rage was far more disturbing to Nancy than her sadness had been, especially when she realized that she felt intense anger toward both her parents and grandparents. It was at this point that the pain in her stomach began to subside. Encouraged, she continued with the LBF process. The more Nancy allowed her anger to surface, the more physical relief she experienced. Also, she became aware of the frustration she felt as a result of her own self-imposed isolation. Although her grandparents had been dead for several years, she continued to live her life as if they were still hovering over her.

Nancy longed to be more spontaneous, to make new friends and move out into the world, but years of overprotection had made her shy and timid. The thought of taking risks or sticking her neck out made her feel weak in the knees. But fueled by the explosive rage she could now direct appropriately, she propelled herself forward.

Nancy regained her health and eventually quit her "sensible" job and went back to school to pursue a degree in literature.

RAGE TERRIFIES

Whereas other intense emotions are uncomfortable to experience, rage is terrifying. It is the "final blow" that pushes us out of control. We feel irrational and panicky in its presence, yet rarely is the degree of our fury equal to the situation. Confronting the painful truth of our unfulfilled desires can create exaggerated and inappropriate responses. A puppy wets behind a chair, and we scream in outrage and slap the child who cares for the pet. We lose our car keys and, in our panic, yell, cry, throw things, or abusively accuse the household or office staff of conspiring against us.

Our belief that rage must be both internally and externally destructive is the result of a lifetime of accumulated frustrations. Incident after incident magnifies our irritation, yet we are unable or unwilling to reveal our true feelings, withholding them even from ourselves. In time our denial results in a prevailing sense of victimization. And because the display of emotion is so unacceptable in our culture, we often compound our fury by feeling guilty or by getting angry with ourselves for being angry. The line between sanity and insanity thins. When the dam breaks, the outcome is often frighteningly unexpected and destructive. We have lost control of our control. Is it any wonder we struggle so terribly to put the feelings of rage back in the now tightly sealed musculature of our bodies?

Rage is especially terrifying to those adults who were abused as children. The experience of having to swallow not only intense anger but also grief, guilt, shame, and fear can make the idea of reconnecting to rage especially threatening. Adults fear not only what their rage might do to themselves but what they might do to others. The sad irony here is that, unless they do learn how to appropriately experience rage, the chances of it either absorbing them or spilling over onto innocent victims is likely. This is not to say that adult victims of physical and emotional abuse cannot appropriately learn to manage their emotions—they can—and they also need to be especially compassionate with themselves.

No one escapes occasional frustration. There will always be those moments when we feel impotent, unable to understand the seeming injustice of life. How we express our frustrations, however, how we experience the feelings of anger and rage, is a choice left solely to us, and it runs the gamut from open acceptance of a personal lesson to ax murder. The child can only flail and scream, but the adult can integrate intellect and feeling. We may feel the same fury we did as tots, but now we can access a dimension of rationality that will enable us to act appropriately and constructively in directing our most intense feelings.

LET RAGE BE YOUR TEACHER

The key to transforming our feelings of rage is to allow ourselves to experience the raw emotion. In order to do this we must take responsibility for our anger while remaining accepting of it. Being closed and critical only turns our fury back upon ourselves; resisting feelings of rage only makes them escalate. Rage is triggered by a sense of victimization and helplessness, but when we fully experience its intensity, we release the energy that allows us to do something about the situation.

All of us have experienced the growing frustrations of a day filled with a series of added irritations. The water heater breaks, you miss an important phone call, you spill mustard on your new pants, your kids spend the morning arguing, you wait an hour to see the dentist, and your car refuses to start. You feel like screaming, your chest feels constricted, your jaw is set, and you think, "If one more thing goes wrong, I'm going to explode!"

But wait! This is the opportunity to really feel your anger and acknowledge it. Feeling it in your body and admitting it to yourself—"God, I'm angry." "I feel angry." "So this is what my anger really feels like"—allow you to begin to release it.

Rage, like pain, is a guide and a teacher. Rage, anger, resentment, and sarcasm can show us where our protections and defenses are the strongest, where we must work hardest. We are given the opportunity again and again to ask, "What am I angry about?" "What threatens me?" "What am I afraid of?" "What basic needs are not being met?" "What am I denying myself—intimacy? nurturing? self-expression?"

An angry remark from parent to son may sound like, "Are you going to get a haircut soon or do you like looking like a Pomeranian?" But it may really mean, "I'm afraid I won't appear to be a good father, that I have lost control." When your wife asks, "Honey, do you really want another drink?" and you explode, hurling the glass against the wall and bellowing, "Yeah, but where no one nags me," and slam out of the house, are you actually saying, "I'm scared. Could I really be an alcoholic? Will she stick by me?" Beneath the surface of rage lies a fear so frightening to consider that we transform the feeling directly into rage, sadness, grief—any emotion that is more easily dealt with and more socially acceptable.

THE RELATIONSHIP BETWEEN
ANGER AND SADNESS

Chronic anger is frequently a disguise for sadness, despair or grief. Chronic anger or rages that go on and on, or are triggered by "a drop of the hat," are forms of protection that frequently mask feelings of vulnerability. In this culture the stereotypic "man" is permitted, even encouraged to be angry. "Anger is aggressive and therefore manly." Sadness, on the other hand, is "weak and feminine." You may not buy the stereotypes—I don't— but that doesn't mean you are not influenced by them.

As you do the LBF process you may discover that your feelings of anger change to those of sadness and the reverse. As long as you ride the feeling that is most intense you will remain "on track."

ANGRY—WHO ME!

People have a variety of excuses for refusing to become angry: "My parents were always yelling, and I swore that I would never behave like that." "No one raised their voice in my house when I was a kid." "People won't like me if I become angry." "I don't like myself when I'm angry." "It's not loving or spiritual to become angry." Sometimes the denial of anger hides a dark and terrible family secret. People are afraid to face frustrations and irritations because they don't want to reveal the "not so nice," "not so loving," "frightening" side of themselves or their families. Nevertheless, when clients ask, "Will others still love me?" I answer, "Can you love yourself hiding from parts of yourself or pretending to be someone you are not!'' Ron's story is typical of those who have found the courage to face themselves and their anger.

Ron was a soft-spoken very, very nice man who always wore a broad smile. He was one of the few people in the AIDS groups who unfailingly had wonderful things to report about his family. He told us that everything about his childhood had been "perfectly wonderful" and the same was true of his life today. He felt only love for others. Anger, according to Ron, simply had no place in his life. In group, Ron was cheerful but critical of other people's anger, disappointment, or discontent. All they really needed to do was, "open their hearts as he had and everything would be okay."

As nice as Ron was, after about three weeks of obsessive pleasantness, the rest of the group was ready to muzzle him and told him so in no uncertain terms. Ron was deeply hurt. He had seen his role in the group as a loving, helping, supporter of others, and he had been unappreciated for his efforts. Ron came back the following week very upset, and I suggested that all of us focus on our feelings by doing the LBF Process. Ron was terrified! He had not allowed himself to experience hurt or anger for many years. The mere thought of rage seemed particularly overwhelming. We listened attentively to Ron as he described his fears and encouraged him, nevertheless, to pursue the experience. Ron consented to feel his rage for "one minute" and came through the process shaken but energized and relieved to find that he had not gone mad or died. The following week Ron returned to the group very excited and told the following story:

That evening as he was driving to group he slowed down to let another car pass. The driver in the car behind him honked and flashed an obscene gesture in Ron's rear mirror. At that point the light changed and they both had to stop their cars. Typically Ron would have swallowed his outrage, but this time, recognizing that he was angry, he turned around in his seat and just glared at the other driver. To Ron's amazement the man was so intimidated that when the light changed he timidly pulled around Ron's car as fast as he could and drove off. Ron felt great having asserted himself. In fact, this delight in his own anger triggered others in the group to ask if he had intended to get physical with the rude driver. Ron replied by saying that he had found the experience of allowing himself to be angry personally invigorating but as far as the other driver was concerned, he had only intended to communicate his outrage. He had no intention of hurting or punishing the other driver. When we allow ourselves to have our feelings doing something about them loses its charge.

RECOGNIZING THE DIFFERENCE BETWEEN EMOTION AND ACTION

I would like to stress that experiencing feelings of rage and anger does not mean that we must act them out. In fact, if we fully permit ourselves to process the feelings as they arise within our bodies, we ensure that the behavior that follows will be appropriate to the situation.

Acknowledging deep-seated rage and anger puts us in touch with life-threatening problems, shows us the futility of our denial, and informs us of our energetic potential for positive and constructive action. Unlike a drowning man who fights the water until he succumbs, we learn to relax and flow with the tide in order to rise to the surface and stay on top.

Eventually you will come to trust staying open even in

the face of emotional storms, at first during the exercises and later through the ups and downs of daily living. Anger and frustration will no longer be so devastatingly frightening. You will not have to wait until the last straw forces you into a confrontation; you will stay current with each new situation; you will make your anger work for you, not against you.

When you stop using your will and emotional strength to push your rage into unconsciousness, power and energy are released. A potential for creative action fills the spaces that were occupied by tightness and tension; and, like any other intense emotion, rage comes to be experienced as an internal guide to well-being.

RAGE INVENTORY

Quickly, without mulling over your answers, circle your feeling responses, remembering that once again this is simply an exercise in information collecting. Answers are neither right nor wrong, good nor bad.

1. People who are very angry are out of   T   F
   control.
2. Intense anger is childish.   T   F
3. Rage is bad.   T   F
4. Intense anger is immoral.   T   F
5. It makes me angry to see someone else   T   F
   getting angry.
6. It frightens me when I feel rage.   T   F
7. It frightens me when people get angry   T   F
   with me.
8. When I feel rage, I hold it inside.   T   F
9. When I feel very frustrated, I cry.   T   F

10. When I feel angry, I yell.   T   F
11. When I feel angry, I take it out on my   T   F
    family.
12. When I feel rage, I get a headache.   T   F
13. When I feel very frustrated, I escape from   T   F
    the feelings by drinking, eating, watch-
    ing TV, meditating, smoking, etc.
14. I was never permitted to show rage as a   T   F
    child.
15. I feel angry most of the time.   T   F
16. I often feel like having a temper tantrum.   T   F
17. When someone blows up at me, I run   T   F
    away.
18. I never get angry.   T   F
19. When I'm angry, I often say things I don't   T   F
    mean.
20. I don't let anger build up inside of me; I   T   F
    deal with it as it happens.
21. Anger is ugly.   T   F
22. Spiritual (religious) people never get an-   T   F
    gry.
23. I feel guilty after I have been mad at   T   F
    someone.
24. Showing my rage makes me feel pow-   T   F
    erful.
25. It's okay for me to get angry and express   T   F
    it.
26. Women never get intensely angry.   T   F
27. Rage excites me.   T   F
28. It takes me a long time to get over my   T   F
    anger.
29. It's okay to use drugs to get rid of anger.   T   F

30. It is difficult for me to express anger directly to a stranger.	T	F
31. I yell and scream a lot.	T	F
32. I find it easier to get angry with those people who are closest to me.	T	F
33. I like to hurt people verbally when I'm angry.	T	F
34. My parents were often angry with me.	T	F
35. When I feel rage, I can stop it with a few drinks.	T	F

MY FEELINGS ABOUT ANGER

Fill in the blanks with the first words (don't use more than two) that come to mind.

1. It makes me feel _____ to see someone angry.
2. I'm afraid to make people angry with me because they will _____ me.
3. People who feel rage are _____.
4. The parent I felt the most rage from was my _____.
5. In my family, rage was usually expressed by _____.
6. When I feel rage, I use my anger to _____.
7. I can stop feeling rage by _____ or _____.
8. When I feel frustrated, I blot out my feelings by _____.
9. The best way to handle rage is to _____.
10. If I got angry enough, I could _____.
11. When I feel angry toward someone I love, I _____.

12. When I feel angry toward someone I barely know, I _____.

13. When my mother was angry with me, she _____.

14. When my father was angry with me, he _____.

15. The most frightening thing about rage is _____.

EXPLORING MY RAGE

1. Do the Living Beyond Fear Process using an enraging experience as your focus. If as you begin to experience the intensity of your felt rage you go numb, uncritically shift your focus to an intense exploration of what non-feeling feels like. (You may wish to refer to Chapter 10, "Numbing.").

2. If you are too agitated to lie down or sit quietly as you follow your breath to the source of intensity within your body, take a walk, run, or hike up a mountain; repeat the first exercise while "moving." Let the rhythm of your movement guide your breath and bring it to the spot in your body that holds the most rage. Keep the focus on your body; do not make this an intellectual exercise. Delete judgment and criticism. If you tire or stop, do not stop breathing or focusing on the feeling.

3. If you tend to unconsciously diminish your breathing as your emotional intensity rises, try this: Tap or press on your chest as a reminder to continue breathing steadily as you proceed with the exercises. Do this any time you feel the need to be reminded.

4. After you have spent time focusing on the raw feeling of rage, ask yourself the following questions. Answer them as fully and spontaneously as possible. Try not

to think about your responses; just allow whatever surfaces to have expression.

- Could this rage be covering up my feelings of sadness, grief, or fear? How far back can I remember feeling this emotion? Allow any images, sounds, voices, that come up to be accepted as helpful and healing information. Let the images play themselves out.

- Do I remember anyone who also felt this way or made me feel this way? Who or what is the source of my rage? What would I like to say to this person or thing?

CHAPTER 10

Numbing

*"You must feel everything, otherwise
the world loses its meaning."*
—Carlos Casteneda

The story of Rip Van Winkle, the fellow who fell asleep for twenty years, is a popular folktale. Everyone can identify to some extent with the theme of sleeping one's life away. In this day and age, turning off has, in fact, become a national pastime.

We have become enormously clever—ingenious, in fact—at devising brilliant schemes to turn off our emotions and tune out physical sensations. We have created myriad ways to silence, numb, deaden, and withdraw from our feelings. The irony, however, is that these strategies, originally intended to protect us, now have become habituated, compulsive, and, in some extreme cases, even lethal.

We work and play under headphones, drive with a telephone in one hand or enveloped in elaborate stereo systems, and snap on the television as soon as we walk through our front doors. Out comes the food, the alcohol, the dope as we binge, drink, and drug ourselves out of loneliness and isolation and into semiconsciousness. We sleep too much, get sick too often, chatter endlessly, move, drive, and work ourselves relentlessly in a frantic attempt to shut out sadness, grief, rage, and fear. We push ourselves to the edge of sanity rather than allow ourselves to be aware of what we feel within. In short, we pretend to live. Instead of enthusiastically experiencing life, we shun it like a lepers' colony, all the while searching almost desperately to find new ways to block out what we cannot forget or forgive—namely our feelings.

EXCHANGING A FULL PALETTE FOR A FEW GRAY TONES

When we first choose not to feel, we're invariably too young to realize that what we're doing is exchanging the full palette of sensations for a few gray ones. Non-feeling is a result of shaving off the peaks and valleys of emotional intensity. It is, at best, an experience of flatness, of sameness, of uniformity, a life of white bread and boiled potatoes. But at the very edge of non-feeling is a subtle, barely perceptible tinge of emptiness and sadness that is ever present. It is a distant memory, a dim recognition that keeps reminding us that something is missing, something is wrong.

To protect ourselves from what we fear, we have maimed our emotional selves by shutting down and, as a result, have dramatically diminished our capacity to experience life—to see, hear, taste, touch, and smell. In so doing we have stunted our sensitivity, creativity, productivity, and vitality. We have narrowed our minds and closed our hearts.

Numbing is also a response to overwhelming feelings of rage or sadness that stem from hopelessness and helplessness. If we believe that no one listens or cares, we may decide to stuff our feelings. If we do this early in life, we can remain habitually shut down long after the circumstances that created the numbing response have passed.

Depression, the feeling of no feeling, chronic distraction, or chronic unexplainable lethargy or exhaustion are obvious indications that we may be numbing. There are also less apparent signs. Benign activities that we pursue in order to avoid our feelings are also numbing strategies. It's all very good to devote ourselves to other people or good causes, or cultural and intellectual development, but when we do these "good things" in order to avoid "bad feelings," we are behaving in an obsessive and compulsive manner that will exhaust and deplete us. Activities that are healthful and life enhancing are also predictably energizing.

NUMBING IS A RESPONSE TO BEING OVERWHELMED

Fear is another source of physical and emotional shutoff. I have pointed out that most of us are ill prepared for experiences that involve us in death and dying. When this is the case and we are forced to come face to face with death, numbing often occurs.

Ted, a young man who I worked with, had an experience that might have overwhelmed anyone. He had volunteered to help out at a hospice for dying AIDS patients and had been assigned to a patient he closely identified with. The relationship between the patient and his aged parents reminded Ted very much of the relationship that existed in his own family. One day Ted arrived to find the old couple anxiously attending to their son who appeared to be on the verge of death. They had been at the hospice all night and most of the day. Ted compassionately suggested a break. He told them that he would help watch while they left the room in order to have something to eat. They gratefully accepted his offer.

No sooner had the old couple left, however, when the son died. Ted was stunned. He had received no training for responding emotionally to such an event. Here was a man he identified with but scarcely knew, who had just died as he stood by watching. Ted could hardly fathom what had taken place. What was he supposed to do? Could this also happen to him? What was he going to say to the old couple when they returned? Ted went numb with the intensity of emotion and confusion, and he stayed that way until he began to reconnect with his feelings.

Numbing is such a powerful process that it not only drains the person blocking their feelings but anyone and everyone in close proximity to some degree. It takes so much energy to completely shut out rage, grief, or fear, that others are also touched and drained by the effects this process has on us. This is especially true of children whose parents habitually numb their feelings. Health-care professionals speak of such children as "carrying or expressing their parents numbed feelings." Numbing in the workplace is contagious and a frequent cause of burnout. Health-care professionals who work in settings characterized by emotional denial experience a level of stress that often tips the balance leading to burnout.

Arlene was one of the most energetic and creative graduate students I ever had the pleasure of working with. She was a hospital social worker who was especially interested in serious and chronic diseases. In returning to school for her doctorate in psychology, she hoped to find a key to the professional burnout she was experiencing. She was clever, very hard working, dedicated, and delightful to be around. No matter how discouraging or difficult a problem, Arlene always managed to lighten it. She cared for and deeply respected the people she worked with and, because she so often felt effective, she loved the work itself. However Arlene hated the attitude of emotional denial that characterized her professional relationships within the institutional setting. Instead of acknowledging the vulnerable emotions that are unavoidably stirred within a crisis setting, feelings were expressed in the form of infighting, quarreling, and backbiting.

Arlene had hoped that by earning a Ph.D. and qualifying for a senior position in the hospital, she could change the emotional environment; but this was not the case. The more she interacted with staff at the institutional level, the more drained and exhausted she felt. Arlene could remain enthusiastic and motivated working with people's pain, fear, or dying processes. But she could not cope with individuals who stuffed their feelings and insisted that feelings were ''unprofessional''—but then covertly expressed their grief, fear, or rancor by fault finding and infighting. She changed jobs twice, trying to find a setting that would feel supportive instead of draining. Finally, after several years she gave up and took a consulting job in the business world where she said she was at least "well paid.".

NUMBING CAN BE LETHAL

People who withdraw have numbed themselves; they have made arrangements and accommodations; they have companions, acquaintances, sex partners. They do not have soul mates, intimates, or lovers. Unfortunately, the sacrifices we make to protect ourselves prove worthless in the long run. Our feelings refuse to be muffled. Life and health demand that we pay attention to the messages they convey. In spite of our efforts to silence them, these messages grow louder and stronger until, eventually, they force themselves to the surface. By then the cost of denying them often is devastating. As we attempt to devise increasingly elaborate defenses, they consume more and more of our energy and health. In time, the distinction between a living process and a dying process becomes so fine as to be nonexistent. At this point, I believe, it is easy to succumb to serious illness.

I had a friend, Jerry, who died of cancer. He was nineteen. Jerry's life story was very much like that of several other people I have known and with whom I have worked. All were quiet, withdrawn, and emotionally dead. Shortly before his death, Jerry wrote a touching story about how having cancer had evoked the emotions he had all but forgotten. His story began with a description of himself before he became ill. He created a picture of a tall, gangling boy whose nose was always buried in a book. During recess and lunch periods, he sat off to the side, reading. He was always alone, whether at home with his family or at the beach with his friends. He did not know how to express his feelings; he barely knew they existed. Jerry wrote of listening to the diagnosis of his cancer without feeling any emotion whatsoever. It was not until later, when he was told that the medical intervention had not succeeded in halting the progression of his disease, that the tears and emotions within him finally surfaced.

Jerry's surgery and his subsequent first round of radiation and chemotherapy had passed by as if they were happening to someone else. But during and after the intensely difficult days of his second round of therapy, when he euphemistically described himself as ''coughing in Technicolor,'' he found within the pages of a journal a friend who could feel his pain and understand. This friend was simply the vulnerable, lonely, and intensely sad boy whom Jerry had so long ago locked away from consciousness. To his delight, Jerry found that this friend could also laugh and play and nurture him.

Jerry wrote voluminously, delighting in the fact that, for the first time in his life, he was able to express all that he felt. He submitted an article that was published in the school paper. In it he told of finding this wonderful lost part of himself because of his having cancer.

When I am with individuals like Jerry, and I have been with many of all ages, I ask myself, Is this what it takes to open people to the fact that they have hidden, locked away, or forgotten a treasure of incalculable value—their feelings? Do they always have to be taken to the precipice before they are willing to confront who they are? In the end, the most life-threatening feelings are the consequence of the decision not to feel. Life is a process that never stands still, never levels off. The decision to feel, no matter how painful or frightening, is a decision to extend our lives. The decision to numb, to withdraw, to escape, is one that undermines this intention.

Again the questions surface: What do you do with your numbness after you have spent a lifetime manufacturing it? Can you really deal with the discomfort of intense emotion? How do you integrate emotion into your life once you find the high and low notes? Believing, at last, that as an adult you can simply handle them is an enormous first step. Know that your feelings, no matter how deadened or denied, are still there. Just because you have not heard the notes does not mean the instrument will not play.

NOT FEELING IS A FEELING

The key is to treat the experience of non-feeling exactly as I have suggested you treat the experience of intense feeling, that is, to simply observe throughout the day your non-feeling response from a perspective of understanding and compassion. If you have turned off, you had good reasons for doing so. Be gentle with yourself, but persist every day for several weeks.

Choose a time of day when you are usually alert to begin the LBF process. Sit in a straight-backed chair, or even walk if you find yourself repeatedly falling asleep. When you're using the time you have set aside for the process, focus on the place in your body where the numbness is most obvious, and breathe into this area. Continue to focus on the center of your deadness. Shaking or trembling may occur as unfamiliar sensations begin to surface. If this happens to you, allow it. The shaking won't harm you in any way and, indeed, is a sign of progress.

Resist the temptation to think about or analyze the situation. Of course, your attention may wander; but each time it does, gently bring it back to the same area of your body on which you have chosen to concentrate. Do not expect miracles. It has taken you a long time to develop the habit of shutting out feeling, and it will take time to learn new patterns. But you will experience changes within a few weeks if you consistently practice the process.

The following is an outline of the LBF process as it applies to numbing. Non-feeling is often more terrifying than any intensely felt emotion, but the process for releasing non-feeling is exactly the same. First locate the place in your body where you feel the greatest emptiness. Often it is the chest, stomach, or pelvis, but it can be anywhere. Take your time as you breathe steadily and deeply into the part of your body that feels the emptiest. Continue to breathe steadily into this area, focusing all your attention there. Follow your breath to this spot during the entire time you have allotted for this exercise. If your mind wanders, gently bring it back, again and again, if necessary. Let the experience of emptiness deepen and intensify.

Know that each time you set the intention to experience your "emptiness" you come closer to discovering the depth of feeling and energy that lies within you. Eventually, as you continue to focus on your body, your trust in it and in yourself will grow. Your fear of being overwhelmed by fear and loneliness or of losing control will give way to confidence and acceptance.

NUMBING INVENTORY

The following questions suggest ways in which you may be numbing and hiding from yourself. Let your physical and emotional feelings direct the responses you give as you keep in mind that here once again is another information-collecting process. Circle the answer that best describes how you feel.

1. I get sick often. T F
2. I have great difficulty expressing anger. T F
3. I always have a drink when I get home T F
   from work.
4. My meals rarely satisfy me. T F
5. I almost never feel sad. T F
6. I watch television several hours each day. T F
7. I rarely feel loving. T F
8. I love the feeling of exercising and mov- T F
   ing.
9. I have close friends. T F
10. Reading is my only pastime activity. T F
11. I am an observer in life rather than a par- T F
    ticipant.
12. I enjoy a good cry occasionally. T F
13. I have a gratifying sex life. T F
14. I rarely feel vulnerable. T F
15. If I concentrate for a moment, I can be T F
    aware of almost any part of my body.
16. Nothing in life seems to excite me. T F
17. I need medication to help me sleep. T F
18. I am depressed frequently. T F
19. I can't get through a day without drink- T F
    ing or using drugs.

20. I have a reputation for being "cool."　　T　　F
21. My energy level is usually low.　　T　　F
22. I have never felt grief.　　T　　F
23. I often feel empty.　　T　　F
24. I breathe shallowly most of the time.　　T　　F
25. I rarely seem to enjoy life.　　T　　F

Fill in the letter code of the word that best applies (N = Never, R = Rarely, S = Sometimes, F = Frequently, A = Always).

1. I'm _____ aware of how my body feels.
2. I _____ feel healthy and strong.
3. I _____ smoke when I'm nervous.
4. I'm _____ in pain physically.
5. I'm _____ able to express my feelings of anger.
6. I _____ use alcoholic beverages.
7. I _____ enjoy having sex.
8. I feel tired _____.
9. I _____ get enough exercise.
10. I _____ feel upset with myself.
11. I _____ felt warm and loved as a child.
12. I have _____ felt grief.
13. I _____ feel good about myself.
14. I _____ sleep well.
15. I _____ feel empty.
16. I cry _____.
17. I _____ feel love.
18. I _____ feel afraid.
19. I _____ feel vital and alive.
20. I'm _____ aware of my feelings.

EXERCISES FOR EXPLORING NUMBING

As you engage in these exercises, remember that your goal is awareness. Change will follow automatically as perception, unencumbered by criticism or judgment, steadily grows.

GAINING INSIGHT ABOUT NUMBING

1. If you grow angry, frustrated, or frightened in the process of experiencing your numbness, begin to direct your focus to the feelings that have presented themselves and breathe into these feelings.
2. If you have become aware that you use food, alcohol, television, whatever, to numb your feelings, try the following procedure: The next time you would like to do something compulsive or inappropriate in order to numb your feelings, focus on the feelings that provoked this urge.
3. Become an uncritical observer of the ways you numb yourself throughout the day. Notice what you do with intense feelings as they arise, and try to find out precisely how you discount or disguise them.

"SOCIALLY ACCEPTABLE" NUMBING

Do you use such things as prayer, meditation, good deeds, or helping others to escape experiencing your own feelings? Become an impartial observer of your spiritual or selfless activities and take note of the following:

1. Can I be flexible with these activities? Can I miss a day now and then, or can I occasionally spend less time on them?
2. Do I pursue these activities in order to numb my feelings?
3. Do these activities energize me?

PART V

Awakening

CHAPTER 11

Life After Fear

> *"To conquer fear is the beginning of wisdom."*
> —Bertrand Russell

A young Zen monk asked his master, who was chopping wood, "Master, what did you do before your enlightenment?"

The old man replied, "I chopped wood."

The young monk thought for a moment and then continued, "Well, then, what did you do after your enlightenment?"

His master's eyes twinkled: "I chopped more wood."

Life after fear is transformational; yet from outer appearance little may seem to have changed except that feelings are experienced rather than numbed or avoided. You will still "lose it" occasionally, act impatiently, upset yourself over petty things, make a fool of yourself, act inconsistently, and feel victimized by backed-up toilets, acid rain, and the telephone company. You never will live beyond error; every day you will demonstrate your lack of total perfection. But the absolute glory of it all, the delicious irony, is that everything you feel will be perfectly acceptable. Your feelings will neither limit nor control you.

That old bogeyman anxiety will also remain a part of your life, but it will be the part that has changed the most. Instead of being a wearying and relentless drain, fear will become an austere but respected friend whose presence communicates change rather than overwhelming you. Feelings of fear will signal that once again you have found the courage to push the limits of your growing edge and confront that which is challenging, unfamiliar, and unknown.

FEELING AWARENESS HELPS US TO BECOME FOCUSED SELF-HEALERS

The ability to experience feelings enables us to be remarkably sensitive to our state of health. Awareness of physical and emotional sensations heightens our perception of what is taking place within our bodies and acts as a guide for gauging well-being. This sensitivity enables us to discern what is health promoting and what is not. It is also an aid in determining which health-care program or combination of health options most effectively supports healing.

The more frequently you check your feelings the more accurate you will be. Bodily sensations are dependable guides for evaluating the relationship between our energy level and such things as food, exercise, and life-style. Feelings are also reliable advisors for determining a variety of health-related issues including how active to be, whether a particular relationship is supportive or not, how hard to push oneself, or when it is time to make a change. People who enjoy a finely tuned connection to their bodies also become active partners with the health-care professionals that serve them. They can, for example, give accurate and specific accounts of the effects of various treatments or report that a prescribed course of treatment is not producing the desired effect.

A finely tuned relationship with our physical and emotional feelings is also an accurate and dependable measure of well-being. The wisdom of our bodies can guide us in selecting the health program or regimen that is best suited to our individual needs. When one is sensitive and finely attuned to feeling sensations, we can ask and get input to very specific questions: ''What is the best of all possible health options for me at this time?'' ''Would acupuncture help boost or preserve my immune system?'' ''Is this chemotherapy, prescribed drug, AZT, etc., supporting my well-being at this time?'' ''Does this particular exercise program, diet, therapy, or practice, further or retard recovery for me at this time?''

Certainly we can and should use our heads to organize and gather information, but only our bodies can provide timely and specific information about the physical feelings and energy levels that reflect our current state of health. Time and again I have come across self-aware and sensitive, feeling individuals who have been able to make successful health-care decisions that were unique and individual. I must caution that I have also seen an equal number of people make unorthodox health-care decisions that were unsuccessful. My belief is that the key to success or failure lies in the sensitivity an individual has to his or her own body.

Sensitivity to one's feelings also enhances our freedom

of choice. The more information we gather, the more there is to choose from. The abundance of data that becomes available when we consult our feelings as well as our thoughts greatly extends our range of choice and thereby our freedom of choice. This advantage insures flexibility and enables us to be more responsible, self-respecting, and in charge of ourselves. It is enormously empowering to feel that we have many options and to know that to some degree we are in a position to positively affect our health. The following story is a testimonial to this fact.

Cheryl was a gentle young woman with a beautiful head of red hair and three young children. Her mother, grand-mother, and great aunt had all died at an early age of breast cancer, and now a malignant lump had been found in Cheryl's breast. When told about the malignancy, she became completely overwhelmed by thoughts that she too was going to die prematurely. Sobbing, she expressed to me her feelings of victimization as she contemplated "not seeing my babies grow up." Cancer had terrified her all her life, and now that she had finally been diagnosed, she was paralyzed by the images of what she believed was going to happen to her.

Though distraught, Cheryl was able to substitute the LBF process of experiencing her feelings for the obsessive thoughts and frightening images that had occupied her mind. This focus on her emotions revealed that much of the sadness and sense of being overwhelmed that she felt was related to the loss of her own mother for whom she had never fully grieved. As she permitted herself to ex-perience this old grief as well as her current fears, she relaxed and her mind began to clear. She saw that in fact, she had many options. She was an individual, not a statistic, and this gave her hope. While she might be genetically predisposed to breast cancer, she was not its victim. In addition to genetic inheritance, other factors would also play a role in determining the outcome of her life—many of which she could control if she chose to.

Cheryl collected information about the options that were open to her. She carefully selected a specialist that she trusted who advised an aggressive approach including radical surgery followed by a prophylactic course of chemotherapy. Cheryl sought the advice of many other knowledgeable people as well, some of whom had differing opinions. Finally, before she went ahead with the surgery, she paused to consider carefully how she felt about the decisions she was moving toward. In the light of all the data she had gathered, she felt well informed and supported. Thus, from a position of strength, she made her choice and prepared for surgery. In readying herself for the operation, she used visualizations and meditations to relax herself and to prepare for the best possible outcome. The operation went well and she recovered rapidly. Then, knowing that she would be undergoing chemotherapy, she carefully orchestrated the next six months of her life.

Child care was arranged so that she could rest not only on the days following her treatment but every day—not an easy task with three little children. During her private times she did the LBF process, yoga, or just slept   whatever she found most helpful at the time. She also was determined to save the beautiful head of red hair she was so proud of. To this end she insisted on using an ice cap during the chemotherapy treatments. Giggling, she told me that she must have presented quite a sight to the staff with her little headphones tucked under her ice cap. She took great pains to make sure that she was relaxed and receptive at these times and in fact she did succeed in saving her hair.

In addition, Cheryl forced liquids, ate selectively, and looked deeply into the parts of her life that were stressful and less than fulfilling. Here she realized that some important needs were not being met. Until her diagnosis she had not taken time to simply be with herself—something she realized that she very much needed. She also became aware that she felt she occupied a secondary place in her husband's work-oriented life and told him so. He responded by telling her this was not true—she was the most important part of his life! Cheryl persisted and asked her husband to demonstrate his devotion by spending more time with her, which he did.

Each step of the way she paused to note how she felt physically and emotionally. She asked such questions as: "How am I doing?" "What changes or adjustments do I need to make?" "Does my life have meaning and purpose?" "Am I enjoying myself?" By the time Cheryl triumphantly completed her treatment she was anything but a victim. Her interest in life and in others had grown to the point that she resolved to begin some kind of volunteer work in order "to give back some of the abundance she had received from life."

It is also important to note that a finely tuned relationship with our bodies is also necessary when our intention is to remain healthy or avoid illness. The same awareness, sensitivity, and ability to make sensitive choices is just as crucial for preserving good health as it is for recovery.

Feeling experience is also an important and empowering adjunct to all forms of psychological therapy and religious or spiritual practices intended to support health and well-being. Whether we're lying on a couch, sitting in a chair, talking, hitting pillows, breathing rhythmically, visualizing, meditating, or praying, the more connected we are to the feeling sensations in our bodies, the more we will benefit from the therapy or healing practice of our choice.

SUBTLE ENERGY MAY HOLD A KEY TO RAPID HEALING

The ability to process all our feelings and to tap old emotional blocks results in our becoming increasingly able to perceive subtle energetic sensations within our bodies. These subtle messages are related to functions like intuition, but they may some day also enable us to tap extraordinary healing capabilities.

From a physical perspective, psychic healing is simply a swifter version of ordinary recovery. Scientific studies of psychic healing conducted by such respected researchers as Dr. Lawrence Le Shan* have shown it to be identical to conventional healing processes except that it takes place far more rapidly. Psychic healing is not magic; it has never been credited with raising the dead or regenerating severed body parts. It has, however, been shown to rapidly dissolve a growth or halt bleeding.

Psychic healing is also self-healing. It may be initiated through the efforts of another person, "a healer." But the healing itself is something that the healee alone accomplishes. While healing of any sort may appear to be directed from outside our bodies, closer observation points

* Lawrence Le Shan, *The Science of the Paranormal*, Wellingborough, Northamptonshire: Agliarion Press, 1987.

to the fact that this is never the case. The self-healing potential of the healee is potentialized by the action of the healer. The effectiveness of the medicine or the medicine man or woman depends on the patient's ability to receive and to make use of what has been offered.

How might we use the subtle energies in our bodies to tap into the phenomenon of rapid healing? At this point there is little more than speculation about how to connect the two dependably, but the relationship between psychic healing and the level of feeling sensitivity that is developed by the LBF process point to some very exciting possibilities. Fine tuning within our bodies may enable us to reach realms of consciousness that lie outside of time and space and explore processes for igniting rapid healing potentials.

FEELING AWARENESS BRINGS RENEWAL AND LOVE INTO OUR LIVES

The Living Beyond Fear process can produce an integration of mind and body that leads to new levels of perception and understanding in all areas of our lives. From a place where feeling informs decision making, creativity is stimulated, and social wisdom flourishes. The ability to solve problems from a broader perspective is enhanced by being able to see beyond the obvious. At work, at home, alone, or in the company of others, knowledge takes on intuitive dimensions.

As physical and emotional data are added to our informational and reasoning capabilities, we no longer shut down or behave inappropriately in any context because of being emotionally overwhelmed. We may, at times, cry openly, shake in our shoes, or express anger, but doing so will not diminish self-control or undermine self-respect. The process of acknowledging our feelings is energizing, and it is this that renews us and insures that we are on a path of well-being. The more we allow ourselves to experience, the more energized we feel. As sadness, pain, and fear are processed, we experience the boundless resources of our rising vitality and the growth of our self-confidence. The more we allow ourselves to experience, the greater our strength and capacity to feel alive. Rarely do we have any idea of the enormous amount of energy it takes not to feel, not to know, to press into unconsciousness what is painful and frightening. Once this energy is no longer diverted and blocked, it is available for positive, rewarding behaviors.

LOVE SURFACES AS FEAR DISSOLVES

But this is not the end. It is, in fact, the wondrous beginning. There is more to come than you could ever imagine. If fear were a stone you could crack open, inside you would find buried a gem of indescribable worth and beauty—and that would be love.

Matter cannot be destroyed—only transformed. When something dies, something else fills that void. Life moves on. I realize that when you are in a state of fear, it seems implausible, ludicrous perhaps, that love and compassion are housed within you. Yet time after time, whether by choice or force of circumstances you confront your deepest fears—the emotions that remain are joy, gratitude, and love.

I have learned that in order to love, we need not work at loving. There is nothing to do. But we do have to work at acknowledging the painful and frightening emotions from which we hide. This process does not involve destroying the "undesirable" parts of ourselves, as that is impossible. Rather, it demands that we acknowledge, understand, and integrate the very emotions we loathe, that we expose the dark side of ourselves to the light.

Experience has taught me that, as human beings, we have only two ways of being: We either live in love or we live in fear. In fear we remain ignorant, diseased, powerless, and unconscious of the beauty and love inherent in our true nature. To live without fear is to live in love, and to awaken to the unimagined experiences of joy that lie ahead on our journey through life. The best of what we are and the worst—all of it—is a miracle when we live in love.

The following story of a rebellious young man points to the fact that love is frequently uncovered in situations requiring us to confront pain and fear.

Danny did his best to make his quiet, foreign-born parents miserable. Though bright, he directed his best efforts toward being irritating and obnoxious.

One of the few people Danny admired was his next door neighbor Sam, a racing car buff. The old gentleman had befriended Danny and taken him to several car meets. When Danny heard that Sam was gravely ill, he didn't know how to react. He liked Sam a lot but didn't want to get into any "sissy feelings." The truth was that the thought of Sam made him feel a little sick to his stomach and sort of teary. Sam lay bedridden for many months next door to Danny, but Danny couldn't bring himself to visit his friend.

Then Sam took a turn for the worse. Sam's desire was to die at home, but he couldn't afford to pay for the twenty-four-hour nursing care that he needed. His wife appealed to her friends and neighbors for help and they generously rallied to her support. 'Round the clock the neighborhood took turns caring for Sam. Danny's parents were among those who volunteered to take a regular shift, and thus it was that Danny finally crossed the threshold to Sam's house. Once inside, having overcome his fear, Danny was a great help. Sam was happy to see him, and it made Danny feel very good to be needed and appreciated. For several weeks the husky teenager fed, lifted, washed, and comforted the old man.

To Danny's amazement, all of this seemed easy, natural, and uplifting. He wondered why he had been so afraid to come over. Danny's parents as well as the neighbors were even more amazed by Danny's behavior. If someone was unable to make one of the shifts, Danny volunteered and took their place. Was this the sullen, cranky teenager who had been so self-involved and irritating? Danny's relationship with his parents greatly improved, and he started to pay more attention to school and his studies. By the time Sam died, Danny had become a "model citizen" and a respected member of the neighborhood. Sam's dying had given Danny the opportunity to overcome fear and thus connect with the loving, caring part of himself.

A desire to be of service to others is often found in people who have faced and overcome frightening and difficult situations. The flood of joy and gratitude that lies at the other end of experiencing painful and frightening feelings, precipitates caring and a deep desire to give. Service on behalf of others becomes a natural extension of our appreciation and compassionate interest in life and begins to occupy an increasing amount of our attention.

Closer to home, as love replaces fear, all of our relationships grow more loving. Intimacy becomes possible once the need for protections is eliminated. We are willing to risk loving and being loved, sharing our most vulnerable feelings, our secrets and mysteries, and letting others share theirs with us. The terrible isolation that so many experience as the result of numbing or withholding feeling from ourselves and others comes to an end. Once "not feeling" loses its purpose, all that we have invested in it crumbles and is replaced by love.

Our relationships with groups of people also changes. When we don't really know ourselves, we feel lonely and isolated in any group—large or small. Though we work, play, or even pray with others, we can be apart from them. As we grow increasingly comfortable with our body's messages, our experience of the group process changes radically. By experiencing ourselves we begin to experience others, and others begin to experience us. In this way our presence is felt as well as seen.

When I first began teaching the LBF process in group settings, I believed that it would take at least ten to twelve weeks in order for the group to learn the process and begin functioning on its own. However, I discovered that once individual group members were familiar with the exercise—a period of only about three to six weeks—the group as a whole functioned remarkably well. There existed a level of intimacy and openness that I would have expected to have taken years or at least many months to develop. Group or community process is a reflection of individual process, and when people become skilled at experiencing their feelings, the groups that they participate in unify in an extraordinarily short period of time.

Profound social implications are connected to the formation of groups, communities, and nations of individuals experienced in processing their feelings. The health needs of the nation and of the planet are akin to the health needs of persons. Neither the one nor the many can survive when a body is disconnected from its brain or a head separated from its heart. The more whole we become as persons, the more whole our families, communities, and social institutions also become.

The love that is tapped as we live beyond fear is also a bridge to the unfolding of spiritual resources and consciousness. Opening of the heart and selfless service are among the outcomes of a process that connects us to what we feel, but there is more. Once negatively charged emotions no longer block access to subtle interior feelings, we come face to face with experiences that characterize spiritual awakening. The myth of our separateness is finally laid to rest as we experience unity, flow, and connection to everything.

CHALLENGES BECOME OPPORTUNITIES

Once we have faced the frightening realities of the past, it becomes easier to face the frightening possibilities of the future. The more sensitively attuned we are to our feelings, the safer it becomes to stretch ourselves, experiment, and take risks. If we have made an unhealthy or inappropriate decision, we are more likely to recognize it immediately and reverse the decision before damage can be done. Each time we meet the challenge of acknowledging our fear, we grow stronger, more vital, more self-assured. We begin to look for the lessons that will ultimately enhance the quality of our lives. Even pain becomes an opportunity for exploration and growth. Rather than crushing our spirit, it assumes the role of guide, ushering us toward a greater acceptance of life. At those times when our lives are the most difficult, we are provided with the greatest opportunity to further expand the limits of self-awareness. To risk going beyond fear is to go to unimagined levels of love, wisdom, and empowerment.

From the standpoint of day-to-day living, we continue chopping the wood and sweeping the floor, but now we face the challenges of life with a playfulness, enthusiasm, curiosity, and boundless energy that gives purpose and meaning to everything we do. The depth of caring that we have discovered is for life itself and all that it holds. We need only continue our willingness to open more widely, feel more intensely, and see more clearly.

LET IT BE

What we most need to learn we already know. Some years ago I awoke from a dream with the lines of the following poem ringing through my mind, like the lyrics of a familiar song. As I wrote them down in the quiet of that new morning, I was deeply moved, for I found within the lines a message that distilled something essential.

Here were the bones, meat, and essence of so much I had sought to understand. Since that time I have shared the poem with many friends. Now it is my pleasure to share it with you, for in ever so many ways it sums up what I have wanted to say, and I offer it here with the sincere wish that you will find it, as I continue to, a succinct reminder of the rewards connected to deeply and fully experiencing ourselves.

Let It Be

Learn what you feel,
Learn what you want,
Learn what you need,
Learn what you do,
    . . . and become wise.

Quiet the judging,
Quiet the hurting,
Quiet the numbing,
Quiet the dreading,
    . . . and become free.

Rest into rage,
Rest into grief,
Rest into pain,
Rest into fear
    . . . and become loving.

Let it heal you,
Let it teach you,
Let it awaken you,
Let it empower you,
    . . . and be transformed.

Jeanne Sandra Segal

About the Author

For the past twelve years Jeanne Segal, Ph. D., health psychologist, has been actively ivolved as a therapist, lecturer, and trainer in the emotional aspects and spiritual aspects of catastrophic illness. Utilizing her early work with cancer patients and their families at the Center for the Healing Arts as a foundation, she has developed an approach to freeing up the emotional blocks associated with fear, numbing, and other negative emotions. Her process is particularly beneficial for patients with cancer, AIDS or other atastrophic illnesses. It is equally effective for health-care professionals caring for these patients, as well as the lovers, families, and friends of these patients.

Dr. Segal is the director of Santa Monica–based Project Life, which offers no-cost workshps on the Living Beyond Fear Process to individuals who have tested HIV positive.

For further information regarding Jeanne Segal's workshops, seminars, and audio cassette tapes, contact Segal Enterprises, 1250 Sixth Street, Santa Monica, CA 90401, or call 213-395-1532.